Reforming Lives
Rebuilding Economy

#TransformingIndia

Reforming Lives Rebuilding Economy

Vivasvan Shastri
Yesha Bhatt

Series Editor
Arun Anand

PRABHAT PAPERBACKS

Published by
PRABHAT PAPERBACKS
4/19 Asaf Ali Road,
New Delhi-110 002 (INDIA)
e-mail: prabhatbooks@gmail.com

ISBN 978-93-5266-983-7
REFORMING LIVES, REBUILDING ECONOMY
by Vivasvan Shastri and Yesha Bhatt

Edition
First, 2018

Price
₹ 150.00 (Rupees One Hundred Fifty only)

Printed at
R-Tech Offset Printers, Delhi

'A life of dignity for every citizen'

Pt. Deendayal Upadhaya's vision for Bharat

Editorial Note

Transforming India

The idea of 'Transforming India' series germinated a few months ago when we were approaching the fourth anniversary of Narendra Modi led National Democratic Alliance government at the Centre. The responsibility to conceptualise and execute this plan was entrusted to me as Editor of this series. I have been ably assisted by a team of writers and researchers to execute this project.

Initially we planned a series of three books covering the first four years of Modi government at the Centre.

One of the key reasons for doing this series was to objectively assess the performance of this government on various fronts as there seems to be a concerted effort to take the national debate away from issues related to the governance.

For a thriving democracy which has the largest pool of youth in the world, what matters at the end of the day is whether a government has done enough to transform the country which is at the cusp of becoming a super power in the global power structure.

India, today, is an aspirational nation. The expectations from Modi government have been very high. We have tried to do a reality check through this series of books i.e. how Modi government has fared in terms of meeting the expectations of the people of India.

With bold moves like demonetisation and implementation of the Goods and Services Tax, Modi government has taken a huge political risk by attempting to break the status-quo. There are few governments in the history of independent India who have pro-actively used the diplomacy to pursue India's geo-political and economic interests globally by engaging with the leading nations in the world power matrix at equal footing.

The tenure of Modi led government would go down into the history of our country as one of the most interesting chapters which had long lasting impact on the national life and India's global positioning. Thus it was important to document what all this government had done on the issue of governance.

The writers of this series have done commendable work as it wasn't an easy task to take out key events and policies from a huge pool of initiatives taken by this government. We hope that this series would be a ready reckoner for those who want to know what Modi government did in some of the key sectors. This is not an all exhaustive series as we have taken select areas and hence many more areas are left to be covered.

We hope the readers would also be able to use this series as reference material. We look forward to your valuable feedback.

New Delhi **—Arun Anand**
July, 2018

Foreword

According to Pandit Deendayal Upadhyaya, "Freedom in a true sense is not only political but includes economic, social and cultural freedom as well."

Even seven decades after independence, a large part of our population still struggles for economic independence. Although the economy has continued to grow post the reforms of the 1990s, it was neither participative nor equitable. In an equitable economy, all sections of society, especially the poor and the disadvantaged have equal access to opportunities. In a participative economy, people are able to fully participate in the economy as workers, consumers or business owners.

Let me cite an example of a 30-year-old young man from a backward community – Shivraj who works as a house-keeping staff in a swanky apartment complex located in the IT corridor of Bengaluru.

Shivraj would make ₹ 12,000/- a month and wanted to open a bank account to save money every month. Opening a bank account before 2014 was a privilege to a few. Shivraj neither had the documents nor adequate funds to maintain an account. Shivraj along with the author visited multiple banks in the Bellandur area of Bengaluru only to be turned down by every bank – both nationalized and private.

It seemed shocking that even in 2013, two decades after the famous economic reforms of the 1990s, a young man from a backward community was excluded from availing even basic banking services.

According to Dr. C. Rangarajan, Chairman of The Committee on Financial Inclusion, “Financial inclusion may be defined as the process of ensuring access to financial services and timely and adequate credit where needed by vulnerable groups such as weaker sections and low-income groups at an affordable cost.”

Dr. Raghuram Rajan, former RBI governor, defines Financial Inclusion as: “Financial inclusion, broadly defined, refers to universal access to a wide range of financial services at a reasonable cost. These include not only banking products but also other financial services such as insurance and equity products.”

Household financial services can be broadly categorized into 3 groups:

1. Contingency Planning which includes Retirement Savings, Buffer Savings and Insurable Contingency.
2. Access to Credit which includes Business Loans, Home Loans, Emergency Loans and Consumption Loans.
3. Wealth Creation means the ability to invest based on the household’s level of financial literacy and risk perception.

The objective of financial inclusion is to ensure delivery of financial services which include bank accounts for savings and transactional purposes, low cost credit for productive, personal and other purposes, financial advisory services, insurance facilities (life and non-life) to all sections of society.

Even after the nationalisation of banks in 1969, only 58% of households have access to banks as per the 2011 Census data.

A survey done by National Sample Survey Organization (NSSO) revealed the following:

- 51.4% of farmer households are financially excluded from both formal/informal sources.
- Of the total farmer households, only 27% access formal sources of credit; one-third of this group also borrowed from non-formal sources.
- Overall, 73% of farmer households have no access to formal sources of credit.
- Across regions, financial exclusion is acute in Central, Eastern and North-Eastern regions. All three regions together accounted for 64% of all financially excluded farmer households in the country. Overall indebtedness to formal sources of finance of these three regions accounted for only 19.66%.

It is clear that a large part of our population was excluded from participating in our growing economy. They had no access to banking services, no easy means to avail credit. Moreover, whenever this disadvantaged part of our population faced a health crisis in the family, they would most likely go bankrupt.

This financially excluded part of our society had no option but to resort to informal sources of financial services – chit funds and money-lending sharks.

As it was difficult to open a bank account, poor people with meagre daily savings resorted to savings in chit funds. Many of the chit fund managers have since eloped with the life savings of the poor. Money that was painstakingly saved everyday for a daughter's wedding or education was now stolen.

Those who wanted credit fell prey to the money-lending sharks. These sharks would provide loans at rates higher than those even charged by the credit cards. The poor had to work all their life just to pay interest. Paying back the principal amount often fell on their children who were bonded to loans.

The pain of Shivraj and millions like him was felt by someone like them. In May 2014, a son of a poor tea-seller went on to become the Prime Minister of India.

Narendra Modi has since then unleashed a series of integrated reforms that promise to deliver economic freedom to all sections of society.

Mahatma Gandhi coined the word *Sarvodaya*, i.e., rising of all. Pandit Deendayal Upadhyaya advocated the concept of *Antyodaya*, i.e., development should begin from the most disadvantaged section of society which in due course would cover all, i.e., *Sarvodaya via Antyodaya*. This model of development is very different from the western top-down models where development is first experienced by the well-off which then percolates to the disadvantaged sections of society.

Antyodaya is bottom up development, i.e., start by bringing development to the poorest first. Narendra Modi's model of development is *Sarodaya* via *Antyodaya*. In this book, we shall take a look at how the policies of the Narendra Modi government has made our economy both participative and equitable.

It is said that a politician focusses on the next election but a statesman focusses on the next generation. The last 4 years have been transformational as Prime Minister Narendra Modi has chosen to be a statesman. He has put the interests of our people, our society and our nation over electoral politics.

Prime Minister's decisions have been courageous and

with every decision he has aimed to transform the lives of every individual. By transforming the lives of every individual and their family, Prime Minister Narendra Modi has accelerated the process of #TransformingIndia.

In Indian politics, it is indeed rare to see a leader who puts India first, party second and self last. The bold and courageous decisions of this government need to be documented as a part of contemporary history.

This book is a humble attempt by the authors to document the process of #TransformingIndia.

Yesha Bhatt
Twitter: @BhattYesha_

Vivasvan Shastri
e-mail: vivasvan@me.com
Twitter: @VivaShastri
Facebook: https://www.facebook.com/viva.shastri
blog: http://vivabunchofthoughts.blogspot.in.

Contents

1
Jan Dhan Yojana

Financial inclusion is the way the Governments strive to take the common man along by bringing them into the formal channel of economy, thereby ensuring that even the person standing last is not left out from the benefits of the economic growth and is added in the mainstream economy, thereby encouraging the poor person to save, safely invest in various financial products and to borrow from the formal channel when he needs to borrow.

Lack of financial inclusion is costly to the society and the individual. Lack of financial inclusion forces the unbanked into informal banking sectors where interest rates are higher and the available funds are much smaller. Because the informal banking structure is outside any legislative framework, any dispute between lenders and borrowers cannot be settled legally. From a society's perspective, financial inclusion increases the amount of available savings, increases the efficiency of financial intermediation, and allows for tapping new business opportunities.

Adding the common man into the mainstream economy has other advantages as well, on one hand, it helps to inculcate the vulnerable section of the society to save money for its future, take benefits of the economic activities of the country by participating in various financial products like banking services, insurance and pension products, etc., and on the other hand, it helps the country to increase the rate of 'capital formation' which in turn gives a push to the economic activities in the economy by channelizing the money from every nook and corner of the country.

The NDA government led by Prime Minister Narendra Modi made itself committed since the beginning of its term to give special emphasis on the financial inclusion of every person of the country. One of the most crucial of the several steps taken by this government is the Jan Dhan Yojana.

Source: *https://www.pmjdy.gov.in/scheme*

Pradhan Mantri Jan Dhan Yojana was launched by Prime Minister Narendra Modi in his first Independence Day speech on 15 August 2014. The slogan of the Scheme is *"Mera Khata, Bhagya Vidhata"* (it means "My account brings luck to me").

Rama Devi is a resident of a small village Nawadkheda in Uttarakhand. Rama Devi is a mother of 3 young children, who in her spare time helps out her husband at his grocery store. She also has a small piece of land where she grows vegetables and cereals.

Rama Devi is one of those who neither had a bank account nor was aware of the benefits of having a bank account. Rama Devi came to know of the Pradhan Mantri

Jan Dhan Yojana when a local IDBI bank representative approached her. The bank began with educating Rama Devi on the benefits of the Jan Dhan Account, such as earning interest on deposits, credit facilities, insurances, etc. Rama Devi too was very curious to know the benefits of the account as well as that of the RuPay debit card. Rama Devi went on to open Jan Dhan account and today has regular credit and debit transactions in her account.

Not only does Rama Devi have access to banking services for the first time in her life, but her banking and financial knowledge has also increased tremendously.

Rama Devi felt so empowered that she also encourages other villagers to open Jan Dhan accounts. Rama Devi now plans to open a recurring deposit account for all her children.

Rama Devi is a true example of *Sarvodaya via Antyodaya*. Once the benefits of financial inclusion and education reached her, she ensured that others in her village also got the benefits of development.

There are many others like Rama Devi. Davendar Kumar Pal is a poor tailor who lives in the Nisai village in Uttar Pradesh. Davendar used to make money from his daily work and wanted to save money so that he could meet the future needs of his family.

Despite many attempts, Davendar could not open a bank account. When asked as to why he did not get an account opened before this, he replied that "...in all the banks, a lot of documents are needed to get an account opened, but I did not have all the documents..."

Davendar was right. Before Prime Minister Narendra Modi had launched the Jan Dhan Yojana, Know Your Customer (KYC) requirements were often difficult for a poor to meet. With the launch of Pradhan Mantri Jan Dhan Yojana,

Davendar was surprised that rather than he having to chase banks, the banks were now chasing him to open an account.

For the first time in seven decades and more than 50 years after nationalising banks, the poor were now customers for banks.

With simplified KYC norms, it was now easy to open zero balance accounts. Davendar went on to open his first bank account. Even though Jan Dhan Accounts can have zero balance, there is a balance of ₹ 11,111 in Davendar's account. Davendar is now able to make small deposits into his account and build a savings fund for his future needs.

But Davendar did not stop here. He went to encourage all his family members to open accounts as well. *'Sarvodaya via Antyodaya'* was once again seen in action – one person's financial knowledge positively encouraged other members of his family to enter the formal financial system.

We now move to Rajasthan. Gomati Patel is a resident of Jhalara village who is illiterate but a hardworking farmer who makes a daily living by selling milk in the nearby villages. Despite years of hard work, Gomati was not able to save any money.

Gomati got a chance to attend a financial literacy session conducted by the IDBI Bank under the Pradhan Mantri Jan Dhan Yojana. Gomati went on to open a Jan Dhan account. Gomati has so far deposited ₹ 79,000 in her account. With savings in her account, Gomati plans to buy 2 more buffaloes so that she can increase her income. IDBI Bank has also offered Gomati an overdraft facility under the Pradhan Mantri Jan Dhan Yojana, which she can use to grow her framing income.

Gomati now finds it easy to make regular savings. She is also encouraging other women in the nearby villages to start saving and build a fund. Gomati is now learning how the NPS scheme can benefit her.

Pradhan Mantri Jan Dhan Yojana has taken the formal banking system to the doorstep of every poor citizen of our country. It is now easy for the disadvantaged sections of society to participate in the economy. Not only has the financial education level increased but the poor are now able to save and protect their future. They are able to use the overdraft facility to increase their ability to earn. Financial status and financial literàcy lead to a higher standard of living for millions like Gomati, Davendar and Rama Devi.

Not only do the poor and the disadvantaged benefit but also the country. Let us take the example of a tribal village of Sampad in Gujarat. Post the launch of Pradhan Mantri Jan Dhan Yojana, it has been clearly observed that savings of lakhs of rupees, which was earlier kept in the homes, now come to the formal banking channel.

According to Dena Bank, the benefits of Jan Dhan Yojana transcend beyond the benefits of the banking services.

"Yes, both literate and illiterate villagers got benefits of PMJDY, i.e., habit of saving, financial security after death with the use of Rupay card, interaction with bank officials, the financial awareness which boost their confidence to live an independent life. Now a new concept of numeric literacy is being taught in the villages by Bank officials and Bank Mitra which helps these villagers to use banking technology, i.e., Rupay card with asecret PIN (Personal Identification Number). Now villagers are not forced to go to the nearest Dena Bankfor withdrawing or depositing the money as with the help of Micro ATM, both financial (deposit and withdrawal of money) and non-financial transactions (balance enquiry, mini statement, etc) are possible. Even if anybody forgot his/her bank account number, then also transactions can be done with the help of Aadhaar number already entered in the bank account of that person. So, it is an example of perfect village banking."

Let us see how having a Jan Dhan account has helped increase the income levels.

Nabisha Begum from Madurai works as a maid. Her husband is a contract labourer and together they have two school-going children. Before having a bank account, Nabhisha Begum used to hardly save any money due to the spending habits of her family. Lack of financial education and not having a habit to save money for contingency often causes the poor to remain in poverty even after working hard for a lifetime.

Nabisha Begum went on to open a Jan Dhan account and also improved her knowledge of how she could save money. Nabisha opened an account with IDBI Bank. She went on to save ₹ 19,000 and with her savings, she opened a flower shop. Today Nabisha has two sources of income – as a maid before noon and as a part-time flower vendor in the afternoon. Nabhisha plans to use the overdraft facility of her Jan Dhan account to further expand her flower business. As we can see from the example of Nabhisha Begum, financial inclusion and education lead to financial stability.

Just like Nabisha, M. Marivel from Madurai also opened a Jan Dhan account. The next day, he collected his passbook and deposited ₹ 100. There were no other transactions by Marivel. Fate took an ugly twist and at a young age of 42, Marivel died of a heart attack.

When the Branch Manager of the Central Bank of India came to know of Marivel's untimely demise, he collected the necessary documents, such as death certificate, Aadhaar card and bank account details of Marivel's wife and sent them to the LIC of India, Divisional Office, Madurai with a copy to the Financial Inclusion Department, Central Office, Madurai.

Within 48 hours, Marivel's wife received ₹ 30,000, i.e., the complete life insurance claim under Pradhan Mantri Jan Dhan Yojana. Not only is a Jan Dhan account a zero-balance account, but it provides life insurance coverage as well.

All the holders of Jan Dhan account are provided a life insurance of ₹ 30,000. There is no need to sign any document, pay premiums or undergo any medical tests to avail of this insurance. Insurance benefits which till now were restricted to a small section of our society are now available to the less privileged and disadvantaged.

XLRI Jamshedpur branch of the State Bank of India initiated a drive to provide Jan Dhan accounts to migrantworkers. 160 women opened accounts, one of whom was a migrant worker from West Bengal who had lost ₹ 50,000 of her life savings to a chit fund scam. With a Jan Dhan account, her savings are now secure and she manages a healthy balance of ₹ 2,000.

All these cited examples are just a tip of an iceberg. On the inauguration day of Pradhan Mantri Jan Dhan Yojana, 1.5 crore bank accounts were opened. Pradhan Mantri Jan Dhan Yojana has created a created a world record for the most number of bank accounts opened in a week.

Guinness World Records recognises the achievements made under PMJDY. Guinness World Record Certificate says': "The most bank accounts opened in one week as a part of financial inclusion campaign is 18,096,130 and was achieved by Banks in India from 23 to 29 August 2014."

By 7 February 2018, over 31 crores (310 million) bank accounts were opened and over ₹ 745 billion (US$ 12 billion) were deposited under the scheme. More than half of these accounts are owned by women.

As we have seen from these examples, PMJDY has indeed managed to change the destiny of millions of Indians and their families.

Pradhan Mantri Jan Dhan Yojana has been started with a target to provide 'universal and clear access to banking facilities' starting with "Basic Banking Accounts" with anoverdraft facility of ₹ 5,000 after six months and RuPay Debit card with inbuilt accident insurance cover of ₹ 1 lakh and RuPay Kisan Card. As many as 1,767 claims were settled towards accidental insurance to RuPay Card holders under the government's flagship financial inclusion programme – Pradhan Mantri Jan Dhan Yojana (PMJDY) as said by PM on 15 August, 2017. In, next phase, micro insurance and pension, etc. will also be added.

Under the scheme:

1. Account holders will be provided bank accounts with no minimum balance.
2. RuPay debit cards will be issued.
3. Accidental insurance cover of ₹ 1 lakh.
4. After six months of the opening of the bank account, holders will be eligible for ₹ 5,000 overdraft from the bank.
5. With the introduction of new technology introduced by National Payments Corporation of India (NPCI), a person can transfer funds, check balance through a normal phone which was earlier limited only to smartphones.
6. Mobile banking for the poor would be available through National Unified USSD Platform (NUUP) for

which all banks and mobile companies have come together.

Opening a Jan Dhan Account is rather simple. All one needs is two signed photos, no other documents are required. According to an RBI statement; "RBI has issued guidelines dated 26 August 2014, where people who do not have officially valid documents or Aadhaar numbers can still get bank accounts opened by submitting two copies of signed photographs at the bank branch." One of the biggest barriers to opening an account was the availability of documents. Under the Pradhan Mantri Jan Dhan Yojana, this barrier has been done away with.

A study (Bank Accounts For The Unbanked: Evidence From A Big Bang Experiment, May 2017) has shown that PMJDY accounts are increasingly being used actively: "70 per cent of the accounts migrate out of dormancy into active use. Second, activity levels in PMJDY accounts increase over time, a pattern not necessarily seen in non-PMJDY accounts. These findings are especially stark given that non-PMJDY account holders in our sample appear to be much poorer and have transaction sizes that are one order of magnitude smaller. Finally, we find that the active accounts experience significant increases in cash balances. Government direct benefit transfer aids but does not fully explain usage. Overall, the data indicate that the unbanked learn by doing, and increase usage of accounts for transactions, liquidity management, and increasingly, balance accumulation."

Another paper (Who Wants To Be An Entrepreneur?, May 2016) suggests that "Financial development facilitates economic growth by moving workers out of less productive, informal entrepreneurial activity into formal jobs in more productive firms."

An article published in LiveMint highlights the following progress of PMJDY.

"In a 2017 working paper, Georgetown University professor Sumit Agarwal and his co-authors studied account activity in 1.5 million PMJDY accounts from August 2014 to May 2015 (the analysis is ongoing to cover a longer period). While usage started off slowly – 81% of new consumers did not make any deposits in the first six months—individuals tended to become more proficient as their awareness of financial services grew. Within one year, the frequency of remittances and deposit and withdrawal transactions gradually reached the same level as a comparable set of accounts opened before the PMJDY, with a concomitant increase in monthly account balance. Along with demand, the supply of financial products rose as well. The authors found an increase in lending in regions where the PMJDY generated new demand for formal credit.

Yakshup Chopra and Prasanna Tantri, researchers at the Indian School of Business, and University of Maryland professor Nagpurnanand R. Prabhala, in a contemporary study, tracked activity in more than 3,000 PMJDY accounts from August 2014 to October 2016 (prior to demonetisation). Their analysis also found evidence of PMJDY accounts catching up with their counterparts over time, with the differences in usage between both types of accounts shrinking by close to half between the first and the seventh quarter. The average account balance of PMJDY accounts more than doubled in the same period. Similar to the "learning" phenomenon observed by Agarwal and his co-authors, these researchers found that increase in ATM usage among PMJDY account holders surpassed those without such accounts.

Beyond enabling account ownership and the use of

financial services, the PMJDY also facilitated financial inclusion for a variety of demographics. The Overseas Development Institute's Manuela Kristin Günther examined data from several recent rounds of the Financial Inclusion Insights (FII) survey of individuals as well as the 2015 FinScope survey of households in four low-income states, and found that socio-economic hurdles were attenuated: women, low-income individuals, rural residents, and the less educated enjoyed greater account ownership following the PMJDY. Owning an account also appeared to weaken significant constraints like large household size, distrust of financial institutions, and distance to the nearest bank branch.

The PMJDY's ability to tap a deep well of unmet demand for financial services was a common theme running through these studies."

CRISIL Inclusix is a unique index to measure the extent of financial inclusion in India across its 666 districts. It uses a statistically robust, transparent and easy-to-understand methodology, and is based on a modular, scalable architecture.

The all-India CRISIL Inclusix score for India improved to 58.01 at the end of fiscal 2016 from 50.12 at the end of fiscal 2013. According to CRISIL, one of the key factors that contributed to this success was alarge number of accounts opened under the Pradhan Mantri Jan Dhan Yojana.

According to a CRISIL report "Jan Dhan Yojana was the prime driver for high growth in deposit accounts – half of 42 crore new deposit accounts opened between 2015 and 2016 were under Jan Dhan Yojana."

Pradhan Mantri Jan Dhan Yojana has brought about a social and economic transformation in our country. It is a monumental step in achieving Pandit Deendayal Upadhaya's vision for India, i.e., a life of dignity for every Indian starting with the poorest of the poor.

Pandit Deendayal Upadhyaya had defined one metric for development – Antyodya, i.e., did the man or woman at the lowest rung of the ladder benefit? In the case of Pradhan Mantri Jan Dhan Yojana, the answer is a resounding YES.

❐

2
Mudra Yojana

Microenterprises are the second largest employers in our country. There is an estimated 5.5 crore micro enterprises which employ close to 10 crore people. These enterprises have a single owner/proprietor who owns and runs the business. Examples of micro enterprises are small manufacturing units, shopkeepers, fruit/vegetable vendors, truck and taxi operators, food-service units, repair shops, machine operators, small industries, artisans, food processors, street vendors and many others.

Micro enterprises form the foundation of our economy. These enterprises survive and thrive on the basis of their skills and hard work. These enterprises are the engine of our economy and have the maximum potential to create jobs and grow our economy. However, the biggest challenge that most micro enterprises face is access to credit.

Source: *https://www.mudra.org.in*

The biggest bottleneck to the growth of micro enterprises is lack of financial support to this sector. The support from the banks to this sector is meagre, with less than 15% of bank credit going to Micro Small and Medium Enterprises (MSMEs).

A vast part of the non-corporate sector operates as unregistered enterprises. They do not maintain proper Books of Accounts and are not formally covered under taxation areas. Therefore, the banks find it difficult to lend to them. Majority of this sector does not access outside sources of finance.

Till date, micro enterprises have to depend on friends, family or money-lenders to meet their capital needs. As most of the micro enterprises have limited assets, they are unable to get loans from banks. Without a guarantor, loans from money-lenders are available at interest rates of 24-36%.

Paying off loans availed at 24%-36% puts a micro enterprise in a never-ending spiral of debt. Even after a hard day of work, the owner of the micro enterprise has little money to take home after paying interest. The everyday battle of a micro enterprise is just to survive and put food on the table for people working for the micro enterprise. Even after 25-plus years of reform, these micro enterprises cannot think of growth.

In addition to access to finance, the micro finances lack access to entry-level technology and infrastructure.

Antyodaya believes in bottom up development, i.e., development should begin with those at the bottom of the pyramid. For the Indian economy to grow, for jobs to be created, we need to first focus on these micro enterprises. Once the micro enterprises grow, India will grow.

With this aim in mind, Prime Minister Narendra Modi introduced the Pradhan Mantri Mudra Yojana (PMMY) on 8 April 2015. The goal of PMMY was to transform micro enterprises by creating an eco-system that will be provided access to finance.

MUDRA stands for Micro Units Development & Refinance Agency. It is responsible for developing and refinancing all micro enterprises sector by supporting the financial institutions which are in the business of lending to micro/small business entities engaged in manufacturing, trading and service activities. MUDRA partners with Banks, MFIs and other lending institutions at state level/ regional level to provide micro finance support to the micro enterprise sector in the country.

Under the MUDRA scheme, banks, micro-finance institutions and other lending institutions will get capital at low-interest rates so that they can provide loans to micro enterprises at low interest rates.

Micro enterprises can avail loans from ₹ 50,000 to ₹ 10 lakhs under the MUDRA scheme. The guarantor for these loans will be the Government of India. In addition, a MUDRA card will be launched with which a micro enterprise can get access to short-term credit to meet any emergency capital needs.

Let us looks at a few examples of how the MUDRA Yojana has transformed micro enterprises and have provided jobs to many.

46-year-old Kakoli Ghosh from Kolkata inherited her father's business 'Bigyan Jantra Silpa' after the sudden demise of her father. She wanted to grow the business but had no access to capital. Kakoli learnt about the MUDRA loan from a drive done by the United Bank of India. She took a MUDRA loan from the United Bank of India. Kakoli now employs 5 locals in her business. Not only has the Bigyan Jantra Silpa grown, but it has also managed to generate employment for locals which has transformed their lives as well.

Nivedita from Ludhiana started her garments business with one sewing machine. Thanks to the MUDRA loan, she has expanded her business and now has 8-10 sewing machines and employs several people at her firm post the expansion. Nivedita also encourages other micro enterprises like hers to avail of MUDRA loan to increase their business.

Shailendra Kumar from Varanasi has been manufacturing 'Geetanjali' detergent since the last 3 years. Due to the lack of funds, Shailendra could only manufacture 15-20 kg per day. He secured a MUDRA loan of ₹ 5 lakhs and expanded his production from 15-20 kg a day to 1 tonne per day. He also employs more people and after paying local wages, makes ₹ 1000-1500 per day. He also pays back his loan EMIs on time.

Shailendra now plans to expand his business even more. Shailendra's journey from being dependent on money-lenders to becoming independent is truly inspirational.

Anwar Ali was earlier employed with a factory. He heard about the MUDRA Yojana and applied for loan to start his own jute factory. Anwar managed to get a loan within a month and started his own factory that manufactures jute products. Anwar has employed 3 more people at his factory. Anwar showcases his eco-friendly jute products at fairs organised by the government. Anwar claims that his business is completely GST-compliant as well. Anwar's journey from being employed to being an employer showcases how a small loan can bring about transformation in the lives of micro enterprises.

Urmila from Muzaffarnagar in Bihar purchased an e-rickshaw with the help of a MUDRA loan. She now earns

₹ 600-700 daily. From being poor and unemployed to be self-employed with a steady income, MUDRA has enabled the skilled, hardworking poor of India to live a life of dignity.

Vishal Kumar from Rampur, Uttar Pradesh was unemployed. Vishal has skills in sales and marketing but remained unemployed. He was dependent on his family and had no regular source of income. One day Vishal saw an advertisement forPMMY in a local newspaper. Vishal began visiting local banks to know more about MUDRA loans. Vishal went on to secure a loan of ₹ 3 lakhs from Prathama Bank with which he opened a computer stationery store.

Using his sales and marketing skills, Vishal grew his business. Today he is self-employed, independent and has a regular source of income. Vishal is now supporting his family and with his income, Vishal has renovated his house and built a new toilet.

Ratna Deb from Moranhat, Assam was a housewife. Her husband used to work in a private firm on a meagre salary. The family income was not enough to support a family of four with two young school-going children. Ratna had earlier taken a course in baking and used this skill to prepare baked foods as a hobby.

One day her friend placed an order of cake. Ratna's friend also informed her of the PMMY, which enables people to get a loan to start a business. Ratna approached a local State Bank of India branch. The bank manager was impressed with her skills and confidence and approved a loan of ₹ 1 lakh for opening a bakery store.

Ratna's bakery store was off to a good start. Thanks to her good baking skills, her business grew. Ratna now makes a net profit of ₹ 15,000 per month. Not only her income, but her standard of living has also increased. Ratna is now able to support her family thanks to PMMY.

Keya Sarkar from Kolkata was good at designing. With encouragement from family, Ratna stared a business. However, soon she faced capital constraints. Her dreams of setting up a boutique seemed difficult. During one of the campaigns of PMMY by State Bank of India, Keya was advised to apply for a MUDRA loan. She applied and got a loan of ₹ 4 lakhs. Keya is now the proud owner of Suchana Boutique in New Barrackpore. Keya supports 15 women and mentors several young women who want to make a name for themselves in designing. Keya is a living example of Swami Vivekananda's message of 'Be & Make'. With the help of Mudra loan, Keya became an entrepreneur and is now helping other women become independent using their skills.

Madhuri Tamankar from Port Blair had a happy life with a 7 year-old child and a wonderful husband. Life took a tragic turn when she lost her husband to an accident. With no job and a child to take care of, Madhuri started offering services as a beautician. However, she had no capital to open a beauty parlour. One day Madhuri went to a known person to borrow some money, who suggested the availability of loan through PMMY.

Madhuri approached State Bank of India and applied for a loan. With the sanctioned amount of ₹ 40,000, she purchased a galvanic machine, an ozone machine and other raw material needed to set-up a beauty parlour. This is a great example of how someone can use their skills to rebuild their lives post a tragedy with a little help from a MUDRA loan.

Phulwari Devi from Uttar Pradesh has opened a kirana store. Rajkumar Ban kimchandra from Manipur has opened a toy store. Danaram Prajapat has opened a tea stall.

Weavers from Tamil Nadu have expanded their business. Kshama Deb has opened a saree store. Nirmala Lakhara of Bhilwara has opened a bangle shop. Gurjeet Singh has opened a furniture shop. Ankit Gupta from Chandigarh has opened a mobile repair store.

On 11 April 2019, over 100 beneficiaries of the Pradhan Mantri MUDRA Yojana, from across the country, interacted with Prime Minister Narendra Modi at his residence.

During the informal interaction with the Prime Minister, many of the beneficiaries explained how their lives had improved through the use of the MUDRA loans sanctioned to them.

Ms. Kiran Kumari, a beneficiary from Bokaro, Jharkhand, who received a loan of ₹ 2 lakhs, explained how she started her own toy and gift shop. Earlier, she and her husband earned their livelihood selling toys as hawkers. After receiving the loan, she has been able to establish herself as a successful entrepreneur.

Source: *narendramodi.in*

Ms. Munirabanu Shabbir Hussain Malek from Surat received a MUDRA Loan of ₹ 1.77 lakhs. She explained how she took LMV driving training and is now earning ₹ 25,000 per month by driving an auto rickshaw.

Mr. Sijesh P. from Kannur, Kerala worked abroad for 8 years. On returning to India, he worked as a sales manager in a medical unit. He enthusiastically explained to the Prime Minister how he was able to set up a unit to produce herbal tooth powder, thanks to a MUDRA Loan of ₹ 8.55 lakhs. He even presented some samples to the Prime Minister.

Source: *narendramodi.in*

Mr. Salehundum Giridhar Rao from Telangana shared his entrepreneurship story with the Prime Minister. He received a loan of ₹ 9.10 lakhs, which he used to further his dye-casting and moulds enterprise.

Ms. Veena Devi from the Kathua district of Jammu and Kashmir works as a weaver. She received a MUDRA loan of

₹ 1 lakh. She is now one of the leading manufacturers of Pashmina shawls in her area. She presented one Pashmina shawl to the Prime Minister during the interaction.

Mr. Satish Kumar from Jammu received a loan of ₹ 5 lakhs. He was earlier unemployed. Now he has a business of manufacturing and trading of steel products. He shared his experiences with the Prime Minister.

Mr. Viplav Singh from Udham Singh Nagar in Uttarkhand worked with a pharma firm but wished to set up his own business. With the help of a MUDRA Loan worth ₹ 5 lakhs, he was able to start his own business of trading pesticides and fertilisers and has now been able to generate employment for several other persons. He also shared his experiences with the Prime Minister.

Several other beneficiaries also shared their experiences.

The Prime Minister appreciated the efforts of the entrepreneurs who have made good use of the MUDRA Loans. He said that 11 crore people have so far benefited from the Pradhan Mantri Mudra Yojana. He said that one of the aims of this scheme is also to increase self-confidence among the people. He said that so far the conventional thinking has been that employment is generated either in the public sector or in the private sector. This scheme, he said, has helped in the development of the "personal sector", as a means of livelihood and self-employment.

There are 11 crore beneficiaries of MUDRA loans. Till date, loans of ₹ 4.6 lakh crores have been sanctioned. 76% of loan accounts are of women and more than 50% of them belong to SC, ST and OBC communities. It is proposed to set-up a target of ₹ 4 lakh crores for lending in the next year.

Most political analysts and economists have failed to gauge the impact of MUDRA on our society and economy.

This is due to multiple reasons. Firstly most analysts and economists often take a macro view of the economy. Fiscal measures which are driven top down, i.e., centrally are easy to assess using available metrics. Policies which are designed and implemented ground up or are de-centralised in nature are often difficult tomeasure. It is for this reason that many are calling our economic growth as jobless. The reason is that the employment generated by MUDRA does not show up in typical job metrics/statistics. It is estimated that more than 5 crore jobs have been generated due to MUDRA.

Mudra is another good example of *'Sarvodaya via Antyodaya'*. By providing access to credit to micro enterprises, businesses are being set-up, established businesses are growing, the unemployed are getting self-employed and jobs are being created. When 5.5 micro enterprises which support 10 crore people become stronger, our nation will also emerge stronger.

❒

3
Pradhan Mantri Jeevan Jyoti Bima Yojana

Pradhan Mantri Jeevan Jyoti Bima Yojana is a government-backed life insurance scheme in India. It was originally mentioned in the 2015 Budget speech by Finance Minister Arun Jaitley in February 2015. It was formally launched by Prime Minister Narendra Modi on 9 May in Kolkata.

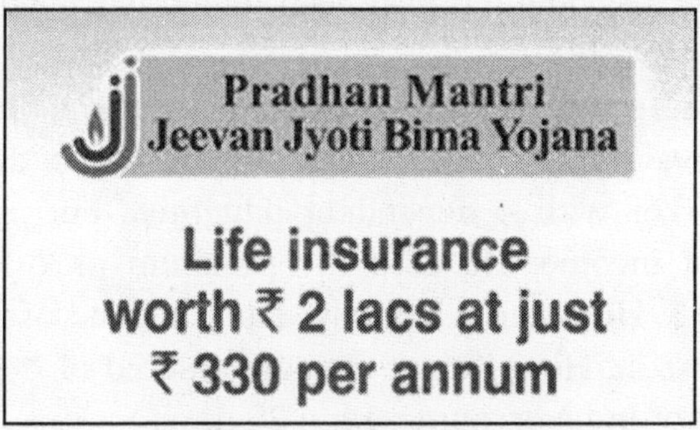

Source: *Ministry of Finance*

Agni Kumar Das from Tripura was diagnosed with a stomach tumour in April 2015. Agni Kumar's family consists of 3 dependents – his wife Dipti Das and two daughters aged 22 and 17 years, respectively. Agni Kumar Das had taken a loan of ₹ 1 lakh from the United Bank of India, of which ₹ 40,000 had been repaid.

On 30 May 2015, Agni Kumar Das had signed up for Pradhan Mantri Jeeven Jyoti Bima Yojana (PMJJBY) by paying a premium of ₹ 330 for life insurance. The very next day he fell seriously ill and had to be hospitalised. He passed away on 1 June 2015, leaving his family with a debt and no funds to support his daughters' education or marriage.

PMJJBY came to the rescue of the Das family. From the 2 lakh insurance of PMJJBY, Agni Kumar's debt of ₹ 60,000 was paid off. The remaining ₹ 1,40,000 was deposited in the accounts for his daughters for their further studies. The elder daughter Shauni Das has taken on the responsibility of running the family by providing tuition services. Agni Das' younger daughter is currently pursuing her Diploma in Electronics and Telecommunication from Tripura Institute of Technology.

Dipti Das has enrolled both herself and her daughter under PMJJBY. She has also been telling her neighbours to enroll for PMJJBY.

From Tripura, now let us travel to Gujarat. Gopal Bhai from Mevalipura village, Savali Taluka was a daily-wage farm worker with 4 dependent daughters but no regular source of income. He paid the premium of ₹ 330 on 4 June 2015. However, a few days later, he died of a massive cardiac arrest. His wife got the sum assured of ₹ 2 lakhs in her Bank of India account within 20 days.

Manish Arora was aware that his father had applied for PMJJBY policy but had little idea about the policy or its benefits. Post the death of his father, Manish submitted all the relevant claim documents. He did not have much hope or expectation from the policybut was surprised to find the sum assured of ₹ 2 lakhs deposited in his account within 30 days. He remains grateful to Prime Minister Narendra Modi for having introduced an insurance product with a low premium but a high sum assured.

Sunita lost her husband and was left to take care of dependent children with no source of income. The only policy her husband had was PMJJBY. A prompt settlement of her insurance claim helped her get back on her feet and live a life of dignity.

P. Srinivasa Rao, an agricultural labourer, lived in Ullipalem village of Krishna district in Andhra Pradesh. Being a poor daily, wage labourer and having no fixed assets in his name, he could barely manage two square meals for his family. He never thought of opening a bank account till he was convinced by Saptgiri Gramin Bank about the benefits of having an account with them. Finally, he opened his bank account in March 2015. With some persuasion from the bank, he also opted for the Union Government's Life Insurance Scheme, Pradhan Mantri Jeevan Jyoti Bima Yojna (PMJJBY) and paid the premium amount of ₹ 330 in July 2015. Suddenly, in August 2015, he got a massive heart attack and died leaving behind his wife and two small kids. His wife knew about the insurance cover her husband had taken under PMJJBY.

She approached the bank for information asking for financial assistance. The bank officials were helpful and assisted her in submitting the death claim to the insurance company which settled the claim in favour of the nominee, wife of the deceased and credited the amount of ₹ 2 lakhs into her savings bank account in November 2015.

With the timely support from the bank and PMJJBY Scheme, the deceased's family got the much-needed financial support and his children could continue their education. We can well imagine the plight of the poor family had the deceased not opted for the PMJJBY. This is an example where a poor family having no assets and fixed income benefited out of the scheme.

Pradhan Mantri Jeevan Jyoti BimaYojana (PMJJBY) is by far the most popular insurance product available in the market today. When the scheme was launched, only 20% of Indians had access to any kind of insurance product.

Majority of the people at the bottom of the pyramid did not have an insurance policy. This was due to multiple factors. Firstly, insurance products were complex and required a lot of documents. Secondly, they were expensive. Lastly, they were not easily available.

PMJJBY is a one-year life insurance scheme, renewable from year to year, offering coverage for death. The cover under PMJJBY is for death only andhence benefit will accrue only to the nominee.

PMJJBY is available to people in the age group of 18 to 50 years (life cover up to age 55) having a savings bank account who give their consent to join and enable auto-debit. The cover is for a one-year period, starting June 1 to May 31.

PMJJBY is designed to address all these issues. It is a term insurance product which provides insurance of ₹ 2 lakhs for a yearly payment of ₹ 330. Anyone with a bank account linked to an Aadhaar card would get a PMJJBY insurance policy. Settling claims werealso made very easy.

Like Agni Das's family, many others have benefited by PMJJBY. As of 24 April 2017, 3.11 crore people have already enrolled for this scheme. 60,422 claims have been disbursed against 63,767 claims received

According to CRISIL, policies such as PMJJBY have played a significant role in improving financial inclusion across the country. ❒

4
Pradhan Mantri Suraksha Bima Yojana

Pradhan Mantri Suraksha Bima Yojana was launched by Prime Minister Narendra Modi on 9 May, 2015 in Kolkata.

A majority of people in rural areas who live below the poverty line have no insurance. Less than 20% of the population of India have insurance of any kind.

With meagre savings and no life insurance, one tragic event can push the entire family into a life of poverty. To address this, on 9 May 2015, Pradhan Mantri Suraksha Bima Yojana (PMSBY) was launched.

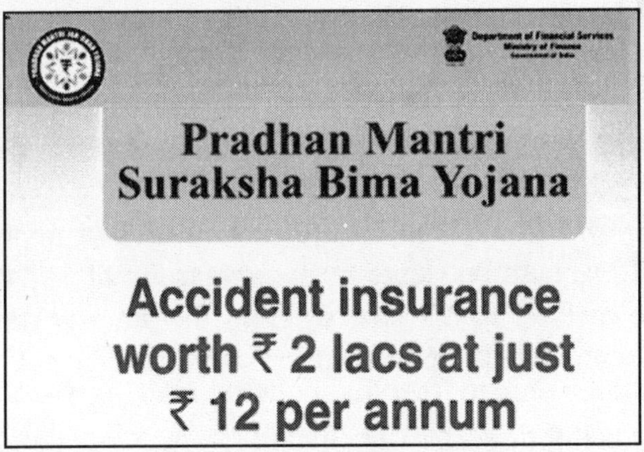

Source: *Ministry of Finance*

Pradhan Mantri Suraksha Bima Yojana is available to people between 18 and 70 years of age with bank accounts. It has an annual premium of ₹ 12 exclusive of taxes. The GST is exempted on Pradhan Mantri Suraksha Bima Yojana. The amount is automatically debited from the bank account.

The accident insurance scheme has one year cover from 1 June to 31 May and offered through banks and administered through public sector general insurance companies.

In case of accidental death or full disability, the payment to the nominee ₹ 2 lakh and in case of partial permanent disability, ₹ 1 lakh. Full disability has been defined as loss of use in both eyes, hands or feet. Partial permanent disability has been defined as loss of use in one eye, hand or foot.

This scheme is linked to the bank accounts opened under the Pradhan Mantri Jan Dhan Yojana scheme.

Suraj, a young man in his twenties, lost both his parents in a tragic accident. He was not only orphaned but now had to take care of his parents' debts. Life seemed to have come to a stop for Suraj. Fortunately, for Suraj, PMSBY policy taken by his parents came to his rescue. With an instant settlement of ₹ 2 lakhs, Suraj was able to clear the family debt and make a new beginning.

As of 24 April 2017, 10 crore people have already enrolled for this scheme. 9,705 claims have been disbursed against 12,975 claims received.

In April 2017, Haryana Government had announced that all Haryana residents in the age group of 18-70 years will be covered by PMSBY, wherein the state government would reimburse the premium to the beneficiary.

The poorest of the poor can now get an affordable insurance product backed by the Government of India.

❐

5
Atal Pension Yojana

The Government of India is extremely concerned about the old-age income security of the working poor and is focused on encouraging and enabling them to join the National Pension System (NPS). To address the longevity risks among the workers in unorganised sector and to encourage the workers in unorganised sector to voluntarily save for their retirement, who constitute 88% of the total labour force of 47. 29 crores as per the 66th Round of NSSO Survey of 2011-12, but do not have any formal pension provision, the Government had started the Swavalamban Scheme in 2010-11. However, coverage under Swavalamban Scheme is inadequate mainly due to the lack of clarity of pension benefits at the age after 60. The new initiative by the Government of India, Atal PensionYojana (APY) addresses the old-age income security of the working poor and the longevity risks among the workers in unorganised sector. It encourages the workers in the unorganised sector to voluntarily save for their retirement. The Government had launched the scheme with effect from 1 June 2015.

Benefits of APY

- Fixed pension for the subscribers ranging between ₹ 1000 to ₹ 5000, if s/he joins and contributes between the ages of 18 years and 40 years. The contribution levels would vary and would be low if the subscriber joins early and increase if s/he joins late.

- The same pension is payable to the spouse after the death of subscriber.
- Return of indicative pension wealth to nominees after the death of the spouse.
- Contributions to the Atal Pension Yojana (APY) are eligible for tax benefits similar to the National Pension System (NPS). The tax benefits include the additional deduction of ₹ 50,000 under Section 80CCD(1).

Atal Pension Yojana (APY) is open to all bank account holders who are not the members of any statutory social security scheme.

Source: *Ministry of Finance*

Any individual who is eligible to receive benefits under the APY will have to furnish proof of possession of Aadhaar number or undergo enrolment under Aadhaar authentication. An APY subscriber will have to get the Aadhaar number recorded in his or her APY pension account and also in his/

her savings account where the periodic pension contribution instalments are debited and government co-contribution is to be credited.

The minimum age of joining APY is 18 years and maximum age is 40 years. Therefore, the minimum period of contribution by the subscriber under APY would be 20 years or more.

The Pension Fund Regulatory and Development Authority (PFRDA) through its 'One Nation-One Pension' Mobilisation Campaign has sourced approximately 3.07 lakh APY accounts, which led to a total of 62 lakh enrolments under the Atal Pension Yojana (APY) as in August 2017.

Under the campaign some of the largest banks in the country, namely State Bank of India helped source 51,000 APY accounts and other prominent banks like Canara Bank which has sourced 32,306 APY accounts, Andhra Bank at 29,057 APY accounts, in other private banks category, Karnataka Bank at 2,641 APY accounts, in RRB's category, Allahabad UP Gramin Bank at 28,609 accounts, followed by Madhya Bihar Gramin Bank at 5,056 APY accounts, Baroda Uttar Pradesh Gramin Bank at 3,013 APY accounts, Kashi Gomti Samyut Gramin Bank at 2,847 APY accounts & Punjab Gramin Bank at 2,194 APY accounts.

The APY Scheme follows the same investment pattern as appliedto the NPS contribution of Central Government employees. During the year 2016-17, it has earned a return of 13.91%.

At the end of Financial Year 2017-18, 97.05 lakh subscribers have enrolled under Atal Pension Yojana. The incremental addition of 48.21 lakh subscribers was 98% more than previous Financial Year 2016-17 figure of 48.83 lakhs. PFRDA appreciates the efforts taken out by the APY

Service Providers (Banks/DoP) for their contribution towards making India a Pensioned Society.

PFRDA has taken various initiatives for the expansion of outreach and ease the operations under APY. Online facility to view Statement of Account and ePRAN card was enabled for easy access of account of APY subscribers. Going ahead mobile applications for empowering the subscribers to view transactions and other details of their APY account was introduced. For the convenience of the subscriber and promoting the digital initiatives of GOI, PFRDA introduced the online registration facility through eNPS Channel by logging in to a website www.enps.nsdl.com without any requirement of a physical document.

At present, 233 Banks and Department of Post are involved with theimplementation of the scheme. Besides the branches of thebanksand CBS-enabled offices of India Post, quite a few banks are sourcing subscribers through their internet banking portals in a paperless environment.

Now APY can also be opened through a complete digital channel through eNPS platform. Currently, 15 banks are offering registration services through eNPS channel including State Bank of India (SBI). A subscriber can view and print the ePRAN card and Statement of Transactions.

Growth of Atal Pension Yojana during the Previous Financial Years

	Number of subscribers	
Financial Year	**Absolute**	**Cumulative**
2015-16	2,484,895	2,484,895
2016-17	2,398,934	4,883,829
2017-18	4,821,632	9,705,461

The highest contributing State is Uttar Pradesh with 11.41 lakh APY accounts followed by Bihar & Tamil Nadu – 8.87 lakh & 6.60 lakh subscribers respectively.

APY Scheme's subscriber base crossed 1 crore on the completion of 3 years of launch. APY was launched on 9 May 2015 and the current number of subscribers stands at 1.10 crore.

Across the country, 1.60 lakhs branches, which include 20 thousand post offices, offer the services of opening APY accounts for their customers. Out of this branch network, nearly 90% of the branches have mobilised one or more APY accounts in the lasts 3 years. Till date ₹ 3,950 crores of contribution has been collected under the APY Scheme. The Scheme has generated around 9.10% CAGR since its inception till March 2018.

This is the aim of many other social security schemes of the Government of India to provide financial security to the common man in case of any untoward and unforeseen situation in life.

We have made immense economic progress, but India is still an uninsured society as a whole. A large segment of the society has been living without any social security or rather an uninsured life. After any untoward incident, i.e., accident or death, every poor family needs financial and social security the most. Social security is an aspect which the present Government identified as a primary need. In order to achieve the objective of social security for a common man, the Government has launched many schemes.

These Social Security Schemes have been launched with the objective of providing insurance services to the economically weaker section of the society. Keeping in mind the lower income group, premiums of these schemes have been kept fairly lowso that the benefit of these schemes can reach far and wide to the unreached. The schemes can be availed via bank accounts only. The Union Government is making tremendous efforts to universalise banking facilities through its financial inclusion scheme.

These Social Security Schemes are leaving a positive impact on the society. State Governments and district administration have been made partners in the implementation of these schemes. There are several success stories of these schemes from the villages and cities. People are not only becoming financially strong, but their life is also changing for good. Their ambitions are growing. This is true financial inclusion in letter and spirit. Corruption is declining as the money is coming directly in the beneficiaries' bank accounts. And this is one of the prime objectives of these schemes. The horizon of a new dawn of social security has set in and more and more people are getting connected to it.

Pradhan Mantri Jeevan Jyoti Bima Yojana (PMJJBY), Pradhan Mantri Suraksha Bima Yojana (PMSBY) and the Atal Pension Yojana (APY) have been launched with an aim to move towards creating a universal social security system, targeted especially for the poor and the underprivileged.

❐

6
Direct Benefit Transfer

Former Prime Minister Rajiv Gandhi had remarked that for every ₹ 1 budgeted by the central government for the welfare and development for the poor, only 16 paise reaches to the poor. This was later confirmed by former Planning Commission Chairman, Montek Singh Ahluwalia in 2009.

When 84% of the funds marked for the development of the poor are being pilfered, it is no surprise that the poor have remained poor after more than seventy years of independence. To ensure that the poor get what is their right, a complete overhaul of the delivery system was required.

Source: *https://dbtbharat.gov.in*

With the aim of reforming our Government delivery system by re-engineering the existing process in welfare schemes for simpler and faster flow of information/funds and to ensure accurate targeting of the beneficiaries, de-duplication and reduction of fraud, Direct Benefit Transfer (DBT) was started.

The three key enablers of DBT are JAM, i.e. Jan Dhan, Aadhaar and Mobile. As on date, more than 22 crore Jan Dhan Accounts, more than 100 crore Aadhaar registrations and about 100 crore Mobile connections provide a unique opportunity to implement DBT in all welfare schemes across the country, including States & UTs.

DBT will bring efficiency, effectiveness, transparency and accountability in the Government system and infuse confidence of citizens in the governance. Use of modern technology and IT tools will realise the dream of MAXIMUM GOVERNANCE, MINIMUM GOVERNMENT.

DBT helps in cutting out middlemen and ensures that subsidies reach the deserving on time. Let us look at how DBT helped Chandigarh become a kerosene-free city and at the same time save ₹ 5 crores in subsidy.

In mid-2014, a survey found that the number of kerosene users in Chandigarh was 62,000. This was a very high number given that even a large city like Delhi did not have more than 1 lakh kerosene users. 35,000 families were drawing subsidised kerosene despite having a LPG connection. Soon the Government introduced DBT for LPG users by linking Aadhaar cards with LPG connections. Thanks to DBT, it was easy to find duplicate users, which was earlier not possible. The Government first made a list of all those registered for LPG subsidies under DBT. Next, they collected the Aadhaar card numbers of ration card holders getting kerosene subsidy.

When the names were compared, it was found that a large number of users were availing subsidies both for kerosene and LPG, which was against the rules. Names of those customers who were availing LPG subsidies were struck off from the list of those eligible for kerosene subsidy. This brought down the number of beneficiaries for kerosene subsidy down from 62,000 to 17,000. The Government, thus, saved ₹ 5 crores and Chandigarh's dependence on kerosene was reduced, which is good for the environment.

In Bihar, the State Health Society has leveraged DBT to implement an Automated Payment Engine to disburse health incentives. More than 90% of payment agencies in Bihar use across all the 38 districts of Bihar. After the implementation of DBT, it is found that average time to receive payments has been reduced by 35% (from 170 days to 111 days). Not only are leakages stopped, but there is a greater transparency and speed in the disbursement of payments.

In Andhra Pradesh, the Krishna District administration is using DBT for paying pensions, making payments under MNREGA, improving quality of service under PDS, making fertiliser distribution more efficient and improving the Nutrition & Health tracking system.

In Madhya Pradesh, over 200 beneficiary-oriented schemes with an estimated budget of ₹ 5000 crores, involving cash or kind benefits, are being run for the welfare of the masses.

The beneficiaries, who are mostly from weaker/under-privileged sections of the society, found it complex and difficult to understand the processes, rules and entitlements of schemes and were not able to get the intended benefits as per their entitlements in a simple and hassle-free manner.

A person was required to have an interface with more than one office and was subjected to repetitive verification of documents.

With the launch of Samagra, a common integrated platform to facilitate a proactive & entitlement-based model of Governance which leverages DBT, benefits are reaching the weaker and underprivileged parts of society.

Till date, 437 schemes across the country from 57 ministries use DBT. The total number of DBT transactions in a year have exceed 5 crores in a year. The total direct benefit transfer now stands at more than rupees three lakh eighty-six thousand crores.

Since 2014, there has been an unprecedented expansion for DBT to the deprived and the deserving. DBT has cut out the middlemen and is putting more money directly in the hands of the beneficiaries. More than anything, there is speed and transparency, for now, it is possible to track every rupee that is being spent.

In addition, the scope for corruption has reduced as it is no longer possible for the middlemen to become rich at the expense of the poor. DBT has transformed service delivery to make it effective, efficient and corruption-free.

❐

7
Annadata – Protecting our Farmers

Pradhan Mantri Fasal Bima Yojana

The weather has not been kind to our farmers over the last many years. After two seasons of drought in 2014 and 2015, we had floods in many parts of the country. Unseasonal rains and hailstorms have also been frequently reported from different parts of the country.

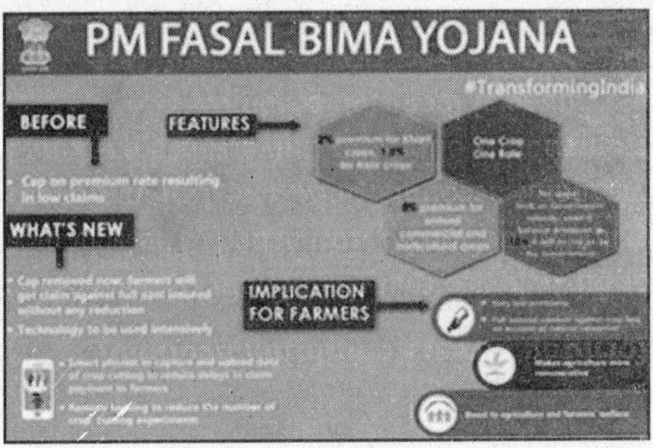

Source: *narendramodi.in*

It is very clear that the UPA era insurance schemes do not provide adequate protection to the farmers. Under the UPA era schemes, i.e., National Agriculture Insurance Scheme (NAIS) and the Weather-Based Crop Insurance Scheme (WBCS), the sums insured were very low. The compensation was very unsatisfying and farmers often had to wait for long and go through a very complex and cumbersome settlement process to get their dues.

At times, the previous Government often used the National Disaster Relief Funds as a stop-gap measure. None of these schemes was based on robust scientific principles and were often interpreted to one's own liking.

To protect the farmers and their incomes from natural calamities which are beyond their control, Pradhan Mantri Fasal Bima Yojana (PMFBY) was launched in April 2016. The Yojana protects the farmers in case of a crop loss due to a wide range of natural calamities, such as droughts, dry spells, floods, inundation, pests and diseases, landslides, natural fire and lightning, hailstorms, cyclones, typhoons, tempests, hurricanes and tornadoes. The scheme even covers post-harvest losses up to a period of 14 days.

The goal of PMFBY was to provide a comprehensive insurance to the farmers with an aim to stabilise and grow their income. With stabilised incomes, a farmer would be encouraged to adopt new and modern practices which would yield to a growing income. Prime Minister Narendra Modi has set a target of doubling the farmer's income by 2022.

PMFBY covers all Food & Oilseed crops and Annual Commercial/Horticultural crops. The premium that a farmer would need to pay is 2% for all Kharif Food & Oilseeds crops, 1.5% for Rabi Food & Oilseed crops and 5% for Annual Commercial/Horticultural crops. The premium rates to be paid by farmers are very low and balance premium will be paid by the Government to provide the full insured amount to the farmers against crop loss on account of natural calamities. There is no upper limit on Government subsidy. Even if balance premium is 90%, it will be borne by the Government.

PMFBY is based on the crop yields. So, if crop yields fall below the threshold yields, based on a seven-year moving average, the farmers would be entitled to making claims. Unlike in the past, the new scheme now removed the subsidy limits. In the original crop insurance scheme, the premiums were capped to contain the subsidy outflows from the centre and state governments. These limits were removed and farmers were entitled to compensation of full claims against crop losses.

Farmer insurance scheme of the past did not cover tenant farmers. In India, a large number of small farmers are essentially tenant farmers. Tenant farmers or sharecroppers are covered under the scheme but would need to provide evidence in the form of a sharing or tenancy agreement for availing crop insurance

In the past, there was only one insurance company that could provide farm insurance – Agriculture Insurance Company of India (ACI). Under PMFBY, 18 insurers including the public sector and private sector companies have been mobilised to implement the scheme.

This scheme removed the previously set cap on premiums so that a farmer can get the full sum assured.

The use of technology will be encouraged to a great extent. Smartphones will be used to capture and upload data of crop-cutting to reduce the delays in claim payment to farmers. Remote-sensing will be used to reduce the number of crop-cutting experiments.

In total, there were 3,66,637 lakh farmers insured in India under PMFBY and RWBCIS (combined) during Kharif

2016. The top 10 states in terms of the number of farmers insured under PMFBY and RWBCIS (combined) during Kharif 2016 were: Maharashtra, Rajasthan, Madhya Pradesh, West Bengal, Uttar Pradesh, Odisha, Andhra Pradesh, Bihar, Chhattisgarh and Gujarat.

The Government of India has recently launched an Insurance portal for better administration, coordination, proper dissemination of the information and transparency for the framers.

An android based "Crop Insurance App" has also been launched, which could be downloaded from the website of Crop Insurance, Department of Agriculture Cooperation & Farmers Welfare (DAC & FW).

According to a report in swarajmag.com

"The results have so far this year been excellent, to say the least. At least, one public sector insurance company, United India Insurance Company has reported claims rate of only 80 per cent or ₹ 1,300 crores during the Kharif and 75 per cent during the Rabi or ₹ 600 crores during the last year, despite 2017's unfavourable weather conditions, natural calamities and drought conditions in parts of Kerala. The losses were far lower than motor insurance, where claims are in excess of 150 per cent. This implied that insurers in the motor sector were paying out claims more than the premiums collected, translating to underwriting losses."

So far, 30% of the farm sector is covered by insurance. The Government aims to increase this to 50% in the coming year. This will not only stabilise the income of farmers but also set a platform from where they can increase their income.

This year, the subsidy outgo to support this scheme is estimated at ₹ 9,000 crores, three times more than the figure in 2015-16.

New Urea Poli.cy

Not so long ago, getting fertilisers at affordable rates was a challenge for the farmers. Farmers had to queue up for days and often struggle to get urea. There was always a demand-supply mismatch which resulted in lack of availability and often a black market. The key reason for this was that government subsidised urea meant for farming was illegally being diverted for industrial use. This caused a massive shortage of urea for our farmers and, at the same time, government subsidy meant for a poor farmer was being misused to generate profit for a few private players.

After assuming office, the Narendra Modi government announced a New Urea Policy, 2015.

The New Urea Policy has multiple objectives of maximising indigenous urea production and promoting energy efficiency in urea units to reduce the subsidy burden on the Government. Savings in energy shall reduce the carbon-footprint and would, thus, be more environment-friendly. It will enable the domestic urea sector having 30 urea producing units, to become more energy-efficient, would rationalise the subsidy burden and incentivise urea units to maximise their production at the same time. The policy will ensure timely supply of urea to farmers at the same Maximum Retail Price (MRP) with alesser financial burden on the exchequer.

It will also reduce import dependency in the urea sector. Urea units would adopt the best available technology in the world and will become globally more competitive. The policy will result in adirect saving of subsidy of around ₹ 2618 crores and indirect saving of ₹ 2211 crores (total savings will be ₹ 4829 crores) on account of revised specific energy consumption norms and import substitution respectively during the next four years. It is expected to result in additional production of around 20 lakhs/MT annually.

The government had also already decided to allow urea producers to produce neem-coated urea up to 100 percent of production and making it mandatory to produce a minimum of 75 per cent of domestic urea as neem coatedso that farmers are benefited. Neem-coated urea is required less in quantity with same plot size and gives higher crop yields. Underground water contamination due to leaching of urea also gets reduced with neem coating since nitrogen in the neem-coated urea gets released to plants very slowly. Neem-coated urea is not fit for industrial use, so chances of its illegal diversion to industries will also be lesser.

By all these measures, import dependency of India for urea is likely to reduce drastically.

In 2017, an interim report prepared by Agricultural Development and Rural Transformation Centre (ADRTC), Bengaluru was released which highlighted the following benefits of the New Urea Policy, 2015:

- Improvement in soil health;
- Reduction in costs with respect to plant protection chemicals;
- Reduction in pest and disease attack;
- An increase in yield of paddy, sugarcane, maize, soyabean and tur/red gram to an extent of 5.79%, 17.5%, 7.14%, 7.4% and 16.88%, respectively;
- Diversion of highly subsidised urea towards non-agricultural purposes negligible among farmers after the introduction of the mandatory policy of production and distribution of only neem-coated urea.

According to Mr. Ananth Kumar, Minister of Fertilisers:

"With neem-coated urea, slow nitrogen release improves soil fertility, which can increase yields by 15-20%. It will also help Government save almost ₹ 5,000 crores."

In March 2018, Government has decided to continue urea subsidy scheme up to 2019-20. The total estimated cost for disbursement of fertiliser subsidy is ₹ 1,64,935 crores. This decision implies that there will be no increase in theprice of urea till 2020.

The decision of the Government has ensured that we have self-sufficiency in the production of urea. There is anadequate supply of urea and neem-coating of urea is mandated to ensure that urea is not illegally diverted and also the yield of the farmers improves.

Prime Minister Krishi Sinchayee Yojana (PMKSY)

India is home to 17% of the world population, 11% of global livestock, but only 4% of world water sources. Water management, hence, becomes a very important part of food security and national security at large.

Source: *https://pmksy.gov.in*

We have a total of 200.8 million hectares of agricultural land in the country, out of which only 95.8 million hectares is irrigated, which is only 48% of the total. Therefore, it is a challenge to provide water to 52% of non-irrigated land and make it suitable for adoption of advanced farming. It's possible only through proper water management. To add to this, we have seen back-to-back seasons of drought in various parts of the country.

To address these issues, Pradhan Mantri Krishi Sinchayee Yojana (PMKSY) has been formulated with the vision of extending the coverage of irrigation – *'Har khet ko pani'* – and improving water use efficiency – 'More crop per drop' – in a focused manner with end-to-end solution on source creation, distribution, management, field application and extension activities.

PMKSY has been approved for implementation across the country with an outlay of ₹ 50,000 crores in five years to develop complete irrigation supply chain, water resources, distribution network and farm-level application solutions to achieve the target of water for every farm. PMKSY is a national mission to improve farm productivity and ensure better utilisation of the resources in the country.

PMKSY Scheme is being implemented in the mission mode with the help of Command Area Development to complete 99 major and medium irrigation projects covering 76.03 lakh hectaresin a phased manner till December 2019.

Ninety-nine irrigation projects which have been incomplete for decades are being accelerated. In the year 2017-2018, 10.13 lakh hectaresof agricultural land has been covered by PMKSY.

Soil Health Card Scheme

With an aim to enable farmers to increase their income and decrease their costs, Government has introduced soil health card scheme in February 2015. Under the scheme, the government plans to test the soil and issue a Soil Health Card (SHC) which will contain the status of the soil with respect to 12 parameters, namely N, P, K (Macro-nutrients); S (Secondary-nutrient); Zn, Fe, Cu, Mn, Bo (Micro-nutrients); and pH, EC, OC (Physical parameters). Based on this, the SHC will also indicate fertiliser recommendations and soil amendment required for the farm.

Source: *https://soilhealth.dac.gov.in*

The card will also contain recommendations for the farmer based on the soil nutrient status. It will show recommendations on dosage of different nutrients needed. Further, it will advise the farmer on the fertilisers and their quantities he should apply, and also the soil amendments that he should undertake, so as to realise optimal yields.

It will be made available once in a cycle of 3 years,

which will indicate the status of soil health of a farmer's holding for that particular period. The SHC given in the next cycle of 3 years will be able to record the changes in the soil health for that subsequent period. Soil samples are taken generally two times in a year, after harvesting of Rabi and Kharif crops, respectively or when there is no standing crop in the field. A sum of ₹ 190 per soil sample is provided to State Governments. This covers the cost of collection of thesoil sample, its test, generation and distribution of soil health card to the farmer. The Government plans to issue the cards to 14 crore farmers.

The scheme aims at promoting soil test-based and balanced use of fertilisers to enable farmers to release higher yields at lower cost. Soil Health Card is prepared in 14 local languages and distributed to the farmers. Now the SHC can be prepared in local dialects, such as Kumaoni, Garhwali, Khasi and Garo.

Against the target of 2.53 crore soil samples, the states have collected 2.71 crore samples and tested 2.05 crore samples to print about 11 crore soil health cards. As of December 2017, 10 crore soil health cards have been issued to farmers.

A study conducted by National Productivity Council (NPC) in 2016 has shown that 84% of farmers have expressed that they have applied the nutrient recommendations suggested in soil health card that has proven to be beneficial to them in reducing the cost of cultivation and improving the productivity of crops.

Soil Health Card mobile app has been launched to help the farmers. The app will benefit field-level workers as it will automatically capture GIS coordinates while registering sample details at the time of sample collection in the field and indicate the location from where the sample has been collected.

This app works like other Geo-tagging apps developed for the Rashtriya Krishi Vikas Yojana. The app contains farmers' details including name, Aadhaar card number, mobile number, gender, address, crop details, etc.

According to Prime Minister Narendra Modi, "Soil health cards had cut the use of chemical fertilisers by 8% to 10% while increasing productivity by 5% to 6%."

National Agriculture Market – eNAM

On 14 April 2016, Prime Minister Narendra Modi launched National Agriculture Market or eNAM.

National Agriculture Market or eNAM is an online trading platform for agricultural commodities in India. The market facilitates farmers, traders and buyers with online trading in commodities. The market is helping in better price discovery and providing facilities for smooth marketing of their produce. The market transactions stood at ₹ 36,200 crores by January 2018, mostly intra-market. Over 90 commodities including staple food grains, vegetables and fruits are currently listed in its list of commodities available for trade.

The eNAM markets are proving popular as the crops are weighed immediately and the stock is lifted on the same day and the payments are cleared online. In February 2018, some attractive features like MIS dashboard, BHIM and other mobile payments, enhanced features on the mobile app, such as gate entry and payment through mobile phones and farmers' database is helping adoption even more. The present trading is done mostly for intra-market, but in phases, it will be rolled out to trade in inter-market, interstate, creating a unified national market for agricultural commodities.

On the eNAM platform, farmers can opt to trade directly on their own through a mobile app or through registered commission agents.

The eNAM is linked with 585 markets (APMCs) in 16 states and 2 union territories, with over 45 lakh-farmer membership in 15 states. The market is helping traders and exporters in procuring quality produce in bulk, at one place and ensure transparent financial transactions.

The Government plans to connect over 22,000 GrAMs, local farmers markets, with the platform. To provide better grading and assaying services, the Agriculture Department is looking at looping in AGMARK for better certification.

An eNAM mobile application is available on Android for farmers and traders to bid and complete a transaction on the app, available in 8 languages.

The payment network RTGS/NEFT, debit card and internet banking was also integrated into the app. In 2017 mobile payment, Unified Payment Interface (UPI) facility through BHIM support was added in the app.

The six States with the most eNAMs as of March 2018 are Uttar Pradesh – 100, Madhya Pradesh – 58, Haryana – 54, Maharashtra – 60, Gujarat – 79 and Telangana – 47.

As of 29 January 2018, agricultural commodities valued at about ₹ 36,000 crores are being traded on e-NAM.

PM Kisan Sampada Yojana

The Central Sector Scheme – SAMPADA (Scheme for Agro-Marine Processing and Development of Agro-Processing Clusters) was approved by the cabinet in May 2017 for the period of 2016-20 coterminous with the 14th Finance

Commission cycle. The scheme has now been renamed as the "Pradhan Mantri Kisan Sampada Yojana (PMKSY)".

It is an umbrella scheme incorporating ongoing schemes of the Ministry like Mega Food Parks, Integrated Cold Chain and Value Addition Infrastructure, Food Safety and Quality Assurance Infrastructure, etc. and also new schemes like Infrastructure for Agro-processing Clusters, Creation of Backward and Forward Linkages, Creation/Expansion of Food Processing & Preservation Capacities.

PM Kisan SAMPADA Yojana is a comprehensive package which will result in the creation of modern infrastructure with efficient supply chain management from farm gate to aretail outlet. It will not only provide a big boost to the growth of food processing sector in the country, but also help in providing better returns to farmers and is a big step towards doubling of farmers' income, creating huge employment opportunities especially in the rural areas, reducing wastage of agricultural produce, increasing the processing level and enhancing the export of the processed foods.

The following schemes will be implemented under PM Kisan SAMPADA Yojana:

- Mega Food Parks.
- Integrated Cold Chain and Value Addition Infrastructure.
- Creation/Expansion of Food Processing & Preservation Capacities.
- Infrastructure for Agro-processing Clusters.
- Creation of Backward and Forward Linkages.
- Food Safety and Quality Assurance Infrastructure.
- Human Resources and Institutions.

Impact of PMKSY

- The implementation of PMKSY will result in the creation of modern infrastructure with efficient supply chain management from farm gate to aretail outlet.
- It will provide a big boost to the growth of food processing sector in the country.
- It will help in providing better prices to farmers and is a big step towards doubling of farmers' income.
- It will create huge employment opportunities, especially in the rural areas.
- It will also help in reducing wastage of agricultural produce, increasing the processing level, availability of safe and convenient processed foods at affordable prices to consumers and enhancing the export of the processed foods.

PM Kisan SAMPADA Yojana is expected to leverage the investment of ₹ 31,400 crores for the handling of 334 lakh MT agro-produce valued at ₹ 1,04,125 crores, benefiting 20 lakh farmers and generating 5,30,500 direct/indirect employment in the country by the year 2019-20.

Minimum Support Price – Budget 2018

A prosperous economy flows from a prosperous agriculture. Agriculture not only provides employment for a large majority of the population, but also provides the means to feed a nation.

But farming is, in fact, one of the riskiest professions as it gets impacted by uncertain weather conditions. Globalisation and trading in commodities havefurther added to the complexity.

A small-time farmer takes on debt and ploughs the field

with a hope of making a reasonable income. An unseasonal shower or a hailstorm is all that it takes to wipe out all the hard work. Even if a farmer gets a good yield for his hard work, commodity prices could fluctuate and small farmers may not even be able to recover their investments. This never-ending cycle of debt has driven many farmers to quit framing. In the worst case, a farmer ends up taking their own life.

People working in the agriculture sector are the largest segment of customers for corporations making consumer goods. When the agriculture economy suffers, a big majority of the Indian population can no longer afford to purchase the consumer goods to meet their needs and wants. The quality of life of the farmer suffers.

To ensure that a farmer gets adequate returns, a minimum support price (MSP) has been established for the farm produce. This would ensure a predictable and a profitable income for our farmers.

MSP also ensures that there is not a big gap between the price of agricultural produce and the industrial consumer goods. Thus, the farmer has the purchasing power to buy the consumer goods to improve the quality of life, and the industrial corporations have a viable domestic market.

The government of India has declared Minimum Support Price (MSP) for crops before their sowing season.

According to a Niti Ayog report:

"The idea behind MSP is to give a guaranteed price and assured market to the farmers and protect them from the price fluctuations and market imperfections. The guaranteed price and assured market are expected to encourage higher investment and inthe adoption of modern farming practices. Further, with globalisation resulting in freer trade in agricultural commodities, it is very important to protect the farmers and their interest."

The MSP also helps the government to procure critical quantities of cereals, which can come to the nation's rescue in the event of food emergency. Through higher MSPs, the government can encourage the production of certain crops to address any demand-supply gaps.

In the 2018 Union Budget, the Government of India announced that the MSP will be increased to 1.5 times their production costs. The biggest beneficiaries of the move will be farmers growing Kharif crops, such as Bajra, Ragi, Tur, Urad, etc.

This is likely to benefit farmers by providing a good return on their investments.

The Government of India have an integrated and comprehensive policy to provide a life of dignity to a small farmer:

- Making farming inputs, such as fertilisers, water and electricity available
- Sharing best practices via DD Kisan channel, advising farmers using soil health cards
- Ensuring a fair purchase price for the produce
- Protecting a farmer by providing crop insurance
- Creating a pan-India market for the produce using technology

Through this integrated policy, the Government of India has ensured that the Annadata of our nation is taken care of. This roadmap laid out by Narendra Modi will ensure that a farmer's income will double by 2022.

❐

8
Ujjwala & GiveItUp

Even today, after more than seventy years of Independence, more than 10 crore homes across India have limited or no access to clean fuel for basic chores such as cooking. The impact of lack of access to clean fuel is most felt by the women and children.

Women frequently have to gather wood for cooking. The process of gathering wood is not only tedious and time-consuming but also not safe. Reports of snake bites and injuries are very common. Burning wood inside homes causes a lot of pollution. This pollution negatively affects the health of women and children causing several respiratory diseases, such as bronchitis, asthma and, in some cases, lung cancer.

As per a WHO report, smoke inhaled by women from unclean fuel is equivalent to burning 400 cigarettes in an hour. According to WHO estimates, about 5 lakh deaths in India alone are caused due to unclean cooking fuels.

The access of LPG cylinders has been predominantly in the urban and semi-urban areas while the poor are still deprived of LPG. Access to LPG continued to be very difficult. It is not very long ago that an Indian family had to use their 'connections' or referrals to get LPG cylinder. Giving bribes to obtain aLPG cylinder was very common. Even those who had a LPG cylinder had to often wait long for a refill cylinder.

Firewood or kerosene stoves were found in most homes as a backup to a LPG cylinder.

Ironically, Government is spending billions in subsidy and every LPG cylinder that we use in our kitchen carries a substantial subsidy. This subsidy was availed by well-off families who did not need it. It was also common to see Government-subsidised LPG cylinders meant for homes being used for commercial purposes such as in a restaurant or for transport.

This translates to a huge annual subsidy burden on the Government, draining precious resources which otherwise could have been used in developmental activities.

Source: *giveitup.in*

Fortunately, many able and aware citizens are not in favour of subsidies and would rather pay the full price for the products and, thereby, they also make a personal contribution towards nation-building. There is a need to spread this message.

Accordingly, the Government has launched the '#GiveItUp' campaign which is aimed at motivating LPG users who can afford to pay the market price for LPG to voluntarily surrender their LPG subsidy.

The process of giving up subsidy was simplified. Earlier one had to visit the LPG distributor and fill up forms. Using its Digital India campaign, a consumer can opt out of availing subsidy by sending an SMS or by using a website or a mobile application.

The critics had anticipated a negative reaction from people for who in their right mind would voluntarily agree to pay a higher price. The critics had under-estimated the ability of Indians to make sacrifices for the greater good of the country.

#GiveItUp campaign received a very positive response with more than 1.5 crore LPG consumers deciding to give up their subsidy.

The Government then plugged any leakages in subsidy using Direct Benefit Transfer (DBT) schemes. Under DBT, the subsidy amount is directly transferred to the Jan Dhan Account, which is, in turn, is linked to the Aadhaar card of the LPG consumer. This prevented any pilferages and also prevented the commercial misuse of LPG cylinders. Getting rid of 3.34 crore fake/duplicate customers allowed the government to save over ₹ 21,000 crores over FY15 and FY16.

With reducing subsidies and DBT eliminating pilferages, the Government focused its attention on the 10 crore women whose life had not changed for the better inmore than 70 years.

Pradhan Mantri Ujjwala Yojana was launched by Prime Minister Narendra Modi on 1 May 2016 in Ballia, Uttar Pradesh. Under this scheme, 5 crore LPG connections will be provided to BPL families with a support of ₹ 1600 per connection in the next 3 years.

Encouragingwomen empowerment, especially in rural India, the connections will be issued in the names of women of the households. ₹ 8000 crore has been allocated towards the implementation of the scheme. Identification of the BPL families will be done through Socio-Economic Caste Census Data.

Pradhan Mantri Ujjwala Yojana has brought about a complete transformation in the lives of women across India.

Source: *http://www.pmujjwalayojana.com*

Before Arti Pal from Panna, Madhya Pradesh got her, LPG connection, she had to use traditional ways to cook. But after receiving LPG connection, she says that now she can cook without any difficulty. She even encourages other women like her to join this scheme.

Neelam Devi, a resident of Kanpur, says that now as she has got her LPG, she no longer have to work in smoke and now can cook very efficiently. Her LPG lasts for one-and-a-half months thus, both money and time is saved. The use of LPG saves a lot of time and, thus, enables women to focus on work as well.

A resident of Valsad, Gujarat says that she can easily manage her work and cooking as cooking on gas doesn't take as much time as the traditional chulha.

Gulshan Jano (aged 32) and her husband are daily wage-workers from Alanpur village, Sawai Madhopur district, Rajasthan. With a new LPG connection, she is happy that she and her children do not have to bear the unhealthy smoke anymore. Besides, she finds it easier and faster to cook using the gas cylinder.

Mrs. Meera Kalita from Bhabanipur, while sharing her story on how PMUY has facilitated her life, says that earlier she had a tough time collecting wood especially during the rainy season and there were times when the family had to stay on fast. It also had an adverse effect on her health as she suffered from eye problem and the smoke would make it worse.

With the tagline, *"Swachh Indhan, Behtar Jeevan"*, the Pradhan Mantri Ujjwala Yojana is aiming to improve quality of life for more than 5 crore women by 2019.

Providing LPG connections to BPL households will ensure universal coverage of cooking gas in the country. This measure will empower women and protect their health. It will reduce drudgery, the time spent on cooking and will also provide employment for rural youth in the supply chain of cooking gas.

Main aim of PMUY: To safeguard the health of women and children by providing them with a clean cooking fuel – LPG, so that they do not have to compromise their health in smoky kitchens or wander in unsafe areas collecting firewood.

Who are the target beneficiaries?

- Under the scheme, five crore LPG connections are to

be provided to BPL households.

- While the selection of beneficiaries would be from the BPL families only, preference would be given to SC/ST and weaker sections of society. While providing the new connections to BPL households, priority would be given to the States which have lower LPG coverage (compared to the national average) as on 1 January 2016.
- The Government has also decided to cover the following categories under the Scheme:

1. All SC/ST household beneficiaries of Pradhan Mantri Awas Yojana (PMAY) (Gramin)
2. Antyoday Anna Yojana (AAY)
3. Forest dwellers
4. Most Backward Classes (MBCs)
5. People residing in islands
6. People residing in river islands
7. Tea & Ex-Tea Garden Tribes

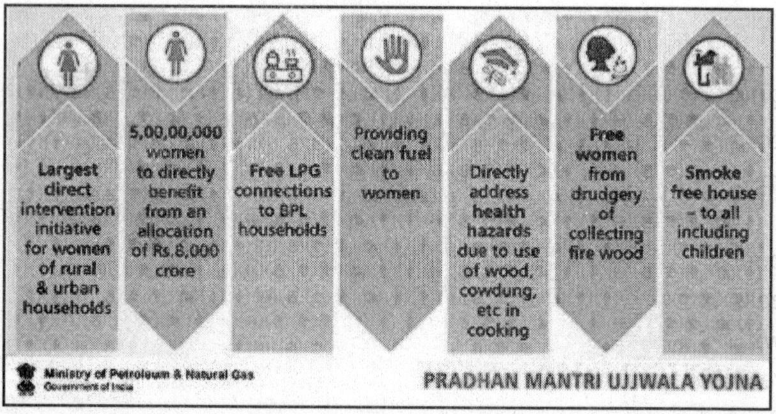

The salient features of PMUY:

- LPG connection is released in the name of the adult

woman of the BPL family.

- The scheme covers the cash assistance of up to ₹ 1600/- for providing new LPG connection.
- The customer bears the cost of Hot Plate and purchase of the first refill. The customers have the option to take Hot Plate on the purchase of first refill or both on loan basis from OMCs at zero interest and the same is recovered through EMIs.
- To ensure smooth supply chain of LPG cylinders to meet the demand, Government is in the process of setting up of 10,000 new distributorships. Majority of these distributorships will come in rural areas to cater to unserved consumers.

In the financial year 2016-17, Oil Marketing Companies (OMCs) have given 3.25 crore new connections. This is the highest ever LPG connections released in any given year. Nearly 80% of households in India now have an access to LPG. 712 districts have been covered under PMUY.

In Uttar Pradesh, the number of LPG connections released as in March 2018 is 64,65,745. In Rajasthan, the number of LPG connections increased from 17,22,694 in 2017 to 26,09,024 in 2018. In Bihar, the number of LPG connections increased from 24,76,953 in 2017 to 48,67,805 in 2018.

Benefits under Pradhan Mantri Ujjwala Yojana have been extended to people of all Hilly States including north east states by treating them as 'Priority States'. This step will effectively address the difficulty faced by poor people residing in the States of Jammu and Kashmir, Himachal Pradesh, Uttarakhand, Sikkim, Assam, Nagaland, Manipur, Mizoram, Arunachal Pradesh, Meghalaya and Tripura in accessing LPG for cooking purposes.

13-14 crore LPG connections were given between 1955 (when the fuel was launched in India) and 2014. This number has swelled to 21.4 crores in the last three years.

All the households would have LPG in the next 2-4 years.

In 2013-14, India had 16.8 crore registered LPG customers, which has increased to 25.37 crores by the end of September 2017. But not all of the registered are active users. As of September, 21.4 crores were active users out of the registered population.

The LPG demand has registered a growth rate of more than 10%. More than 4,600 new distributors have been added in the last 3 years, which have come up primarily in rural belts.

On account of huge response from women, particularly in the rural areas, the target of PMUY is enhanced from five crores to eight crores with an additional allocation of ₹ 4,800 crores which would be achieved by 2020.

The Pradhan Mantri Ujjwala Yojana is a perfect example that shows that the Government does not only announce schemes but is committed to their time-bound implementation. Under the PMUY, the original target was to release 3 crore connections by the end of FY 2017-18, but as a result of efficient scheme implementation and monitoring, more than 3.35 crore connections have been released till date.

LPG panchayats have also been launched to distribute LPG cylinders and educate people about the safe use of clean fuel. Each LPG panchayat would have up to 100 members who have got LPG cylinder under PMUY. It will provide a forum to share their own personal experiences, discuss issues and resolve any myths.

The forum also discusses the benefits of using clean

fuel. The forum also educates people on how clean fuel is good for the environment and is empowering for women. More than 1 lakh LPG panchayats are being planned all across the country.

Source: *Rashtrapati Bhavan*

One such LPG panchayat was held at the Rashtrapati Bhavan by President Ram Nath Kovind.

20 April 2018 was celebrated as Ujjwala Diwas. On Ujjwala Diwas, more than 15,000 LPG panchayats were held. On this day, Ujjwala targets were scaled to cover 8 crores, which would cover 80% of all households who do not have access to clean fuel.

PMUY is likely to result in an additional employment of around 1 lakh and provide the business opportunity of at leastRs 10,000 crores over the next 3 years to the Indian industry. The launch of this scheme will also provide a great boost to the 'Make in India' campaign as all the manufacturers of cylinders, gas stoves, regulators and gas hose are domestic.

PMUY demonstrates that the government is not

shy to take on challenges. It showcases a deep-rooted commitment to develop the weakest and the most disadvantaged parts of our society.

It also demonstrates that the solutions envisaged by the government are integrated, holistic and scalable. PMUY works well with Digital India and DBT which showcases the integral nature of the reform. PMUY encompasses education, adoption of LPG and sharing of practices and is therefore holistic. PMUY was launched with a target of 2 crore cylinders, which, in no time, was scaled to 8 crores.

A nation can transform only when the life of every citizen is transformed. PMUY has for sure changed the lives of rural India for the better.

❐

9
Saubhagya

Even after 70 years of independence, there are more than four crore houses in our country which do not have an electricity connection. The total number of families in India is 20 crores, out of which 4 crores is about 20 percent.

Till today, leave alone the bulb, even electricity could not reach four crore households of the country. Candles, lanterns are still being used in those households. Even today, children in crores of those poor families face problems when they study after evening. Even if they study, they do it in light of those lanterns. the women of these houses also have to cook in the dark and, therefore, most women are under pressure to finish the kitchen work before the day is over. There are no lights in homes, no lights on roads. It is difficult to get out of homes in the dark, especially for women. If the electricity connection is provided to these homes, then only their fortunes will shine.

Under the Pradhan Mantri Sahaj Bijli Har Ghar Yojana, Saubhagya, the government is aiming to give electrical connection to every household in the country, be it in a village or city, be it a shanty or a hut in any remote area.

Prime Minister Narendra Modi launched Pradhan Mantri Sahaj Bijli Har Ghar Yojana – "Saubhagya" in September 2017. It aims to achieve universal household electrification by the 31st of December 2018. The total outlay for the project is ₹ 16,320 crores. The Government of India will provide largely funds for the Scheme to all states/UTs.

Pradhan Mantri Sahaj Bijli Har Ghar Yojana 'Saubhagya'

Life of an average girl Anu in Dampur village of Jaisalmer, Rajasthan revolved around executing laboriously, the daily survival chores. Household chores took a lot of time in the morning. And then she ran for school. By the time she would come home, it would start getting dark. The darkness around her was engulfing her dreams like a venomous snake. Light was nowhere. Candles and kerosene were too expensive for her family. How would she study and take herself forward? Under the scheme, electricity has reached her village. She could study all evening now.

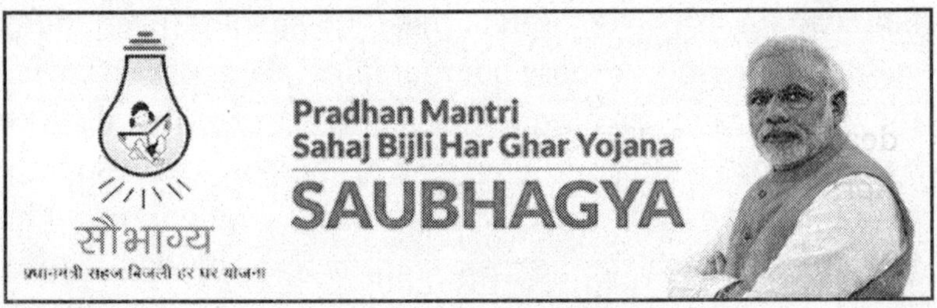

Source: *http://saubhagya.gov.in*

Sumitra Devi of Dheeya, Udaipur, Rajasthan, is delighted that she no longer has to stay at home after sunset. "Earlier we had to finish cooking food before sunset because it is difficult to cook in the dark. Also, since there are lights everywhere, women are not scared to stay out," she says.

Features of Saubhagya:

- Environmental upgradation by substitution of kerosene for lighting purposes

- Improvement in education services
- Better health services
- Enhanced connectivity through radio, television, mobiles, etc.
- Increased economic activities and jobs
- Improved quality of life especially for women

Electricity for all and better quality of life for women:

- Electricity would substitute the use of kerosene which will reduce the indoor population that most of the women are subjected to.
- Lighting after the sunset also provides a sense of enhanced personal safety especially for women and increase in post-sunset social as well as economic activities.
- Household electrification also increases opportunity for women to study and earn.

All villages would be electrified by the scheduled deadline of 1 May, 2018. This target was achieved on 28 April, days ahead of the planned schedule.

The scheme design will rely on the 2011 socio-economic and caste census to identify households that will get free connections along with metering facilities. The households not included in this census data can pay for their connections at a nominal fee of ₹ 500, which the local power distribution company (discom) can claim in ten monthly instalments. For very remote villages, the Saubhagya scheme will provide solar power packs, battery back, with LED lights, and a direct current-driven fan.

The Saubhagya scheme will be run by the Rural Electrification Corporation (REC) as a nodal agency. This is a good decision for two reasons. Firstly, since the REC also owned the electrification of the unpowered 18,542 villages, it has a credible experience of running nationwide electrification programmes in collaboration with state discoms.

Secondly, the REC is a well-managed public sector enterprise (PSE), with high-quality engineering and administration talent, especially in relation to other departmental PSEs.

The Prime Minister also called upon ONGC to use its ₹ 100 crore start-up funds to develop user-friendly electric cooking appliances, saying it would help in reducing the fuel consumption.

The GARV portal indicates that out of the 17.92 crore households in rural areas, 13.87 crore families have got electricity connections. As many as 4.05 crore families are yet to be provided electricity connections.

Saubhagya is an infrastructure creation programme, which is definitely necessary to power up an estimated 250 million Indians who live in the dark today. The poor people will now have Saubhagya (good luck) of having power in their homes.

❒

10
Digital India

Access to the internet is no longer a luxury. It is now a utility just like electricity and water. Digitisation is democratic by nature. It has the power to provide information and connect people. A #NewIndia can only be built by digitising the delivery of government services.

Digital India is a campaign launched by the Government of India on 1 July 2015 and consists of three core components, (a) digital infrastructure as a core utility to every citizen, (b) governance and digital services on demand, and (c) universal digital literacy.

There are 9 pillars of the Digital India programme.

- Broadband Highways
- Universal Access to Mobile Connectivity
- Public Internet Access Programme
- e-Governance – Reforming Government through Technology
- e-Kranti – Electronic delivery of services
- Information for All
- Electronics Manufacturing
- IT for Jobs
- Early Harvest Programmes

To provide internet as a utility to every village in India, the Government of India has decided to provide a minimum of 100 Mbps broadband connectivity to each one of all 250,000 Gram panchayats in the country covering nearly 625,000 villages to transform to Digital India.

The last-mile connectivity with a total of 700,000 WiFi hotspots to cover all 625,000 villages of India, by adding 2 to 5 WiFi hotspots per gram panchayat and minimum one WiFi hotspot per village.

55,619 villages in the country do not have mobile coverage. The Government of India aims to provide universal mobile connectivity to every villager in India at a projected cost of ₹ 16,000 crores.

Accessing government services has never been easy especially for the poorest of the poor. Digital India program aims to digitise government services and make them available to every citizen on their phone.

Using the Umang app, a farmer can now download his soil health card, get the weather forecast, dealer information on seeds, fertilisers, farm machinery and pesticides.

A pensioner can view his passbook. A citizen can pay his road tax and check his vehicle's RC. An aspiring student can find out which all institutions and courses on technical education are genuinely approved by the Government of India. e-Pathshala ensures that education reaches children, teachers and parents. Any student can download Class 1-12 books, education content in audio and video format.

When in crisis and in need of blood, Umang app also helps a citizen check the availability of blood in a blood bank nearby. One can also book OPD appointments within a few seconds using the app. You can check the correct price of medicines using Pharma Sahi Daam.

e-Disha from the Government of Haryana helps in applying, tracking and downloading certificates for Backward

Class, OBC, SC, ST, etc.

Skill India programmes can also be accessed on Umang app. Umang app also has a job portal to search and apply for jobs.

In all, there are 205 government services from 38 departments available on a single app. So far, there are more than 50 lakh users of the Umang app. With Digitisation, a citizen does not need to go anywhere to avail services, for the government has decided to make its services available to every citizen.

As a part of the Digital India initiative, 250,000 Common Service Centres (CSC) will be built across the country, i.e., there will be one CSC centre in each gram panchayat.

As per the Government-owned site csc.gov.in:

"CSCs are the access points for delivery of essential public utility services, social welfare schemes, healthcare, financial, education and agriculture services, apart from ahost of B2C services to citizens in rural and remote areas of the country. It is a pan-India network catering to the regional, geographic, linguistic and cultural diversity of the country, thus enabling the Government's mandate of a socially, financially and digitally inclusive society."

BHIM app named after Dr. Babasaheb Ambedkar was launched by Prime Minister Narendra Modi on 30 December 2016. BHIM aims to facilitate cashless transactions and is based on the Unified Payments Interface (UPI).

BHIM app allows users to transfer money instantly between the bank account of any two parties. BHIM also allows users to check their account balance. Transactions on BHIM are instantaneous and can be done 24×7 including on weekends and bank holidays.

Currently, the BHIM app supports 13 out of the official

22 languages of India. In the near future, it is expected to support all the 22 official languages.

BHIM app is one of the topmost apps on Google Playstore. In the financial year 2017-2018, the BHIM app has been used to complete 913 million transactions with a value of ₹ 1 trillion or ₹ 100,000 crore. BHIM has been more popular than other digital wallets as it directly transfers funds from account to account.

BHIM app has made it very easy for the citizens to operate their accounts and has played a pivotal role in driving India towards a less cash economy.

Since 2014, #DigitalIndia has seen a significant progress:

- Number of smartphones has increased from 22 crores to 40 crores.
- Number of mobile phones has increased from 90 crores to 108 crores.
- Number of internet users have doubled from 24 crores to 50 crores
- Aadhaar – a digital identity has seen growth in registered users from 63 crores to 114 crores.
- United Nations eGovernance index – India has risen 11 positions since 2014.
- 90,966 gram panchayats have been connected.
- 358 km of optical fibre was laid till 2014. Now the figure stands at 2.05 lakh km.
- 1635 institutions have been connected via the National Knowledge Network.
- 87.11 lakh e-signatures issued a 226% increase over 2015-2016.
- Digilocker has 51 lakh users, 79.66 lakh uploaded documents and 171 crore issued documents.
- MyGov has emerged the world's largest digital

democracy platform with 41.79 lakh users, 56 groups, 720 discussion groups and 616 tasks.

- Growth in CSCs from 83,000 to 2.5 lakhs in the last 3 years.
- 82.7 lakh candidates trained under National Digital Literacy Program.
- Pradhan Mantri Gramin Digital Saksharta Abhiyan (PMGDISHA) has made 6 crore candidates digitally literate in 2 years.
- Digital Education – 2,000 courses offering 80,000 training hours.
- Digital Skilling–NIELIT has trained 10 lakh candidates.
- Skill Development in Electronic System and Design Manufacturing has trained more than 2 lakh students.
- eNAM has unified 250 agricultural markets in 10 states with 36.4 lakh farmers and 84,000 traders registered.
- Growth in domestic production of LCD/LED TVs and smartphones.

PM Narendra Modi's ambitious Digital India mission is expected to create over five crore jobs in various sectors. The project will also facilitate training to around 1 crore students for IT sector by 2020 – opening new windows of opportunities for professionals with a host of careers and jobs. This is according to a press release by Timesjobs.com.

The present government is pushing ahead the Digital India initiative to transform the country into a digitally empowered society and a knowledge economy. With the launch of this initiative, the government aims to reach out to citizens in the remotest of locations and make them a part of India's growth story.

❐

11
Skill India

Demographic dividend, as defined by the United Nations Population Fund (UNFPA) means, "the economic growth potential that can result from shifts in a population's age structure, mainly when the share of the working-age population (15 to 64) is larger than the non-working-age share of the population (14 and younger, and 65 and older)."

In other words, it is "a boost in economic productivity that occurs when there are growing numbers of people in the workforce relative to the number of dependents".

UNFPA stated that "a country with both increased numbers of young people and declining fertility has the potential to reap a demographic dividend.

India will be the largest individual contributor to the global demographic transition. A 2011 International Monetary Fund Working Paper found that substantial portion of the growth experienced by India since the 1980s is attributable to the country's age structure and changing demographics.

The U.S. Census Bureau predicts that India will surpass China as the world's largest country by 2025, with a large proportion of those in the working age category. Over the next two decades, the continuing demographic dividend in India could add about two percentage points per annum to

India's per capita GDP growth.

Anis Chakravarty, Lead Economist, Deloitte India, explained that, "India will account for more than half of the increase in Asia's workforce in the coming decade, but this isn't just a story of more workers: these new workers will be much better trained and educated than the existing Indian workforce, and there will be rising economic potential coming alongside that, thanks to an increased share of women in the workforce, as well as an increased ability and interest in working for longer. The consequences for businesses are huge."

However, in order for India to reap the dividends of its demographic potential, it has to first equip its workforce with the necessary skills to contribute to the national economy. Anis Chakravarty further adds, sounding a note of caution, "With the invasion of machines and improvement in robotics, India needs to pay special attention to skilling and reskilling its workforce with a focus on the changing nature of today's jobs. In recent years, India has taken proactive steps to deal with the disruptions in the job market with the 'Skill India' initiative being one of them. That said, it needs to be a continuing process of upgrading skills in a rapidly changing environment."

Deloitte further adds "India, with its abundant human resources, increasing foreign investments and rising disposable incomes, is on its way to becoming a global economic power. However, India needs to take a proactive approach to prepare its workforce for the changing needs of the market, thereby creating a new highly skilled workforce for the ageing world."

Two out of three Indians are below the age of 35. It is estimated that a million Indians enter the workforce every month. At the same time, the industry claims that many of those seeking employment do not have the relevant skills.

Skilling India at scale is the one way to provide quality jobs to a young India and setting a stage for India to emerge as a global emerging power that can provide a highly skilled workforce for the ageing world.

Skill India campaign was launched by Prime Minister Narendra Modi on 15 July 2015 to train over 40 crore people in India in different skills by 2022.

Dinesh Kumar is a young educated man from a poor family. Despite being educated, Dinesh found it hard to find a job. Dinesh got enrolled under the Pradhan Mantri Kaushal Vikas Yojana (PMKVY). In 40 days, Dinesh learnt how to do house-wiring for 2 and 3 BHK homes as well as take care of industrial wiring. Dinesh is now confident of his future thanks to the skills he has acquired.

Abdul Mannan from Rampur, UP–a Pradhan Mantri Kaushal Vikas Yojna (PMKVY) candidate and his successful journey with Aadit Systems. He belongs to a very poor family in Rampur, His father is jobless and unemployed. Due to poor economic condition, Abdul took education only up to 12th class. He came to know about PMKVY scheme through his friend and joined it for Field Technician–Air Conditioner Course. After completion of training, he got an opportunity to join Voltas as a Field Technician. He is now able to help his family and planning to enroll for graduation.

Suman learnt retail skills like customer and business management during her 45 days of training at IL&FS Institute of Skills under PMKVY. She has also enhanced her command over English and gained the confidence to work in biggest retail stores.

Sahil Majhi was unemployed. Son of a plumber, Sahil had dreams of becoming an engineer. He joined the automotive course under PMKVY and learnt how an automobile works. Post completing his course, Sahil plans to open his own automotive repair and maintenance shop.

Sneha Pandey, an aspiring Installation Technician (Computing Peripherals) learnt how to assemble computers and install operating systems and other software products.

Rukhsar from Srinivaspuri, Delhi is a housewife. She wanted to learn and acquire skills but with the responsibility of a young child, she found it difficult to enroll in a course. With the help of courses offered under PMKVY, Rukhsar was able to learn computer basics while also taking care of her child. Rukhsar is now confident to find employment in any office.

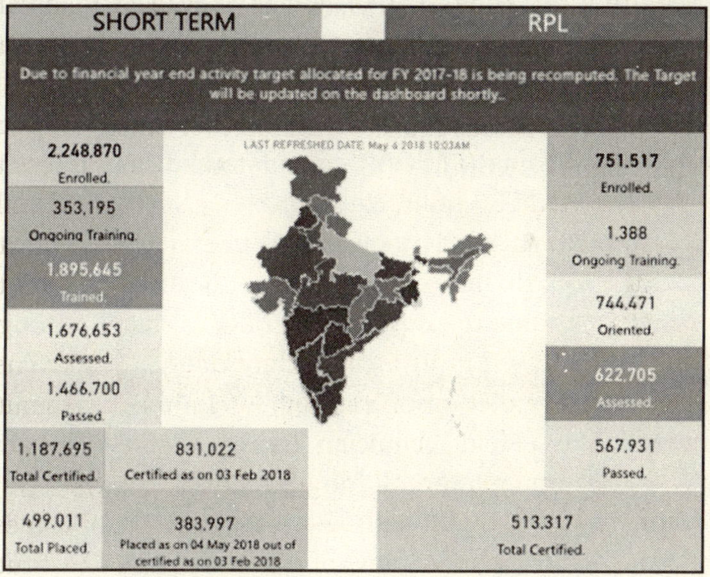

Source: *http://pmkvyoff icial.org/Index.aspx*

PMKVY consists of many components

- Short-term training
- Recognition of Prior Learning (RPL), i.e., certify a

previously acquired skill

- Special projects
- Kaushal and Rozgar Mela
- Placement assistance
- Continuous monitoring
- Branding & communication

India has recently signed an agreement with the UK to work together in the field of skill development. Pandit Deendayal Upadhyaya's philosophy of Integral Humanism advocates that the development of an individual and that of our nation are inter-linked.

A skilled individual can contribute to the needs of the society. Society, in turn, rewards an individual's skills by providing employment and growth opportunities.

In a globalised and ageing world, a young and skilled India will provide the requisite workforce for the development of India and the world.

❐

12
Starup India

Launching a startup is a dream for many entrepreneurs today and the Startup India is a guiding light.

The campaign was first announced by Indian Prime Minister Narendra Modi during his 15 August 2015 address from the Red Fort in New Delhi.

Startup India is a flagship initiative of the Government of India, intended to build a strong ecosystem for nurturing innovation and Startups in the country that will drive sustainable economic growth and generate large-scale employment opportunities. The Government through this initiative aims to empower Startups to grow through innovation and design.

#startupindia

Startup Definition: As defined by Department of Industrial Policy & Promotion (DIPP):

- Startup means an entity incorporated or registered in India
- Up to a period of seven years from the date of incorporation /registration or upto ten years in case of Startups in the Biotechnology sector

- As a private limited company or registered as a partnership firm or a limited liability partnership
- With an annual turnover not exceeding ₹ 25 crores for any of the financial years since incorporation/ registration
- Working towards innovation, development or improvement of products or processes or services, or if it is a scalable business model with a high potential of employment generation or wealth creation
- Provided that an entity formed by splitting up or reconstruction of an existing business shall not be considered a 'Startup'

An entity shall cease to be a Startup:

- On completion of seven years from the date of its incorporation/registration, ten years in case of Startups in the Biotechnology sector, or
- If its turnover for any previous year exceeds ₹ 25 crores

The Action Plan is based on three pillars – Simplification and handholding, funding support and incentives, industry-academia partnership and incubation. Following are the 19 Action Points under the Startup India initiative:

Simplification and handholding

1. Simple Compliance Regime for Startups based on Self-certification
2. Launch of Mobile app and Portal for compliance and information exchange
3. Compliance Regime based on Self-certification
4. Startup India Hub
5. Rolling out of Mobile app and Portal
6. Legal Support and Fast-tracking Patent Examination at Lower Costs

7. Relaxed Norms of Public Procurement for Startups
8. Faster Exit for Startups

Funding support and incentives

1. Providing Funding Support through a Fund of Funds with a Corpus of INR 10,000 crores
2. Credit Guarantee Fund for Startups
3. Tax Exemption on Capital Gains
4. Tax Exemption to Startups for 3 years
5. Tax Exemption on Investments above Fair Market Value
6. Organising Startup Fests for Showcasing Innovation and Providing a Collaboration Platform

Industry-academia partnership and incubation

1. Launch of Atal Innovation Mission (AIM) with Self-Employment and Talent Utilisation (SETU) Programme
2. Harnessing Private Sector Expertise for Incubator Setup
3. Building Innovation Centres at National Institutes
4. Setting up of 7 New Research Parks Modelled on the Research Park Setup at IIT Madras
5. Promoting Startups in the Biotechnology Sector
6. Launching of Innovation Focussed Programmes for Students
7. Annual Incubator Grand Challenge

Startup India Status Report:

Out of the applications received, 6,096 have been recognised as Startups by DIPP. 74 Startups have been approved for availing tax benefits by IMB, as of the 1st week of January, 2018.

COMPLIANCE REGIME BASED ON SELF-CERTIFICATION: Compliance norms have been eased in order to reduce the regulatory burden on Startups, thereby allowing them to focus on their core business.

a) Startups falling under the list of 36 "white" category industries will not require Environment clearance under 3 Environment-related Acts, viz., The Water (Prevention & Control of Pollution) Act, 1974; the Water (Prevention & Control of Pollution) Cess (Amendment) Act, 2003 and the Air (Prevention & Control of Pollution) Act, 1981.

b) Ministry of Skill Development and Entrepreneurship (MSDE) has issued an advisory to states to allow Startups to self-certify compliance for a period of 1 year with the Apprenticeship Rules, 1992 of Apprenticeship Act, 1961.

c) As per the advisory issued by Ministry of Labour & Employment (MoLE) on 12.01.2016, Startups may self-certify compliance under 6 Labour Laws. MoLE has now increased the tenure of compliance of self-certification under 6 Labour laws from 3 to 5 years. 26 states, viz., Andhra Pradesh, Assam, Chhattisgarh, Chandigarh, Daman & Diu, Delhi, Gujarat, Himachal Pradesh, Mizoram, Odisha, Punjab, Tripura, West Bengal, Uttar Pradesh, Haryana, Jharkhand, Madhya Pradesh, Maharashtra, Tamil Nadu, Telangana, Uttarakhand, Rajasthan, Karnataka, Bihar, Andaman & Nicobar and Arunachal Pradesh have confirmed compliance.

STARTUP INDIA HUB: Startup India Hub was operationalised on 1 April 2016 to resolve queries and provide handholding support to Startups. The hub has handled more than 77,000 queries from Startups through telephone, email and Twitter. To seek clarifications pertaining to Certificate of Recognition as a "Startup", Certificate of Eligibility to avail tax benefits, seeking information on incubators or funding, one can get in touch with the Hub on Toll-Free number: 1800115565 or Email ID: dipp-startups@nic.in. The hub has mentored more than 450 Startups for incubation, funding support, on business plans, pitching support, etc. A Startup India Online Hub launched on 19 June 2017 will serve as an online platform where all the stakeholders of the Startup ecosystem can collaborate and synergise their efforts. More than 21,000 users have registered.

PATENT BENEFITS: A Panel of 423 facilitators for patent and design applications and 596 facilitators for Trademarks applications has been constituted for assistance in filing Intellectual Property (IP) applications and to fast-track the process of patent filing and acquisition. DIPP bears the facilitation cost on behalf of Startups and also provides a rebate in the statutory fee for filing an application. Under the scheme for Startups Intellectual Property Protection, Patent applicants have received the benefit of up to 80% rebate in patent fees and free legal assistance. Startups have also availed the benefit of fees rebate in expedited examination filing fees [Form 18(A)]. Trademark Rules, 2017 have been recently amended to provide 50% rebate in Trademarks filing fee to Startups. Overall, more than 970 Startup cases have been facilitated under the scheme.

RELAXED NORMS OF PROCUREMENT

To create a conducive ecosystem for the growth of Startups and provide an equal platform to Startups vis-à-vis the experienced entrepreneurs/companies in public procurement, relaxed norms of public procurement for micro and small enterprises have been provisioned in the Procurement Policy of Ministry of Micro, Small and Medium Enterprises (MSME). Department of Expenditure has also notified that all Central

Ministries/Departments shall relax the condition of prior experience and prior turnover in public procurement to all Startups (whether MSEs or otherwise) subject to meeting of quality and technical specifications. Department of Public Enterprises has expanded the relaxation to Central Public Sector Undertakings (CPSUs). GFR 2017 has incorporated rules which provide for the relaxation of conditions of prior turnover, prior experience and exemption from submission of Earnest Money Deposit (EMD) for Startups.

TAX BENEFITS

Tax Exemption

- The Finance Act, 2016 had made provision for Startups to get income tax exemption for 3 years in a block of 5 years, if they are incorporated between 1 April 2016 and 31 March 2019. In the Union Budget 2017-18, the Government has increased this period of profit-linked deductions available to the eligible Startups to 7 years. To avail these benefits, one must get a Certificate of Eligibility from the Inter-Ministerial Board of DIPP.

Tax Exemption on Capital Gains

- Section 54 EE has been introduced under the Finance Act, 2016 which provides for exemption of capital gain up to INR 50 lakhs arising out of transfer of long-term capital asset invested in a fund notified by Central Government. Also, Section 54 GB of Income-Tax Act, 1961 has been amended to provide an exemption from tax on capital gains arising out of the sale of residential house or a residential plot of land if the amount of net consideration is invested in equity shares of eligible Startup for utilising the same for purchase of specified asset.

Removal of Angel Tax

- Tax exemptions on investments above Fair Market Value have been introduced on 14 June 2016 for investments made in Startups.

FUND OF FUNDS FOR STARTUPS (FFS): A 'fund of funds' of INR 10,000 crores to support innovation-driven Startups has been established, which is being managed by SIDBI. The corpus shall be released over two Finance Commission cycles, by 2025. FFS invests in SEBI-registered Alternative Investment Funds (AIFs), which, in turn, will invest in Startups. INR 600 crores have been released to SIDBI. Total commitments stand at INR 605.7 crores to 17 AIFs. 75 Startups have received funding from various AIFs.

LEARNING & DEVELOPMENT MODULE: Startup India has launched an interactive online learning and development module to educate Startups and aspiring entrepreneurs, through various stages of their entrepreneurial journey. Over more than 1,91,000 applicants have signed up for the course, out of which around 8,000 applicants have completed 100% of the course successfully.

ATAL INNOVATION MISSION: The guidelines for harnessing private sector expertise to set up incubators, organising annual grand challenge for innovative solutions to problems faced by industry and those posed by Ministries as well as the establishment of tinkering labs have been formulated and published on NITI Aayog's and Startup India's website.

ESTABLISHMENT OF TINKERING LABS: As per the

Startup India Action Plan, 500 Tinkering Labs are to be established. NITI Aayog has selected 941 schools for establishing Tinkering Labs. Of the 457 selected in FY2016-17, 374 Tinkering Labs have received a Grant-in-Aid of INR 12 lakh each.

In respect to the establishment of new incubators in institutions as well as in the private sector, NITI Aayog has approved 13 institutes to establish new incubators with a grant of INR 10 crores each. 6 established incubators have received the scale-up grant of INR 2.5 crores as the first instalment. The second round of screening and selection of Atal Incubation Centres (AICs) and Established Incubation Centres (EICs) was held on 2 June 2017.

7 Research Parks will be set up as per the Startup India Action Plan. Research Park at IIT Kharagpur is under construction and INR 74.83 crores have been released. The Research Park at IIT Gandhinagar is being set up by DST which has sanctioned INR 90 crores and disbursed an initial instalment of INR 40 crores. The remaining 5 are being set up by Ministry of Human Resource Development (MHRD) and DST at IIT Guwahati, IIT Hyderabad, IIT Kanpur, IIT Delhi and IISC Bangalore. In addition, another Research Park at IIT Bombay is under construction and INR 34 crores have been released.

PROMOTING STARTUPS IN THE BIOTECHNOLOGY SECTOR: Under Biotech Equity fund, INR 1 crore each to be given to bio-incubators. 3 bio-incubators have been selected as recipients of the above-mentioned Equity Fund. A total of 30 bio-incubators have been supported (sanctioned amount of INR 185 crores) by DBT. The impact has been multi-fold as a total of 290 Startups have received benefits from these bio-incubators.

TECHNOLOGY BUSINESS INCUBATORS (TBIs) AND STARTUP CENTRES: The objective is to propel successful innovation through augmentation of incubation and R&D efforts. 15 TBIs and 15 Startup centres are being set up. 11 TBIs have been approved and other 4 are in advanced stages. Funding amount of INR 3.75 lakhs for each of the 10 Startup centres has been released by MHRD as a 1st instalment of the grant. Funds for the other 5 Startup Centres areat various stages of approval.

INR 42 crores have been sanctioned and INR 17 crores have been disbursed already to 11 TBIs.

UCHCHATAR AAVISHKAR YOJANA (UAY): The objective of UAY is to promote industry and outcome-oriented research projects by students. INR 475 crores for 2016-18 have been earmarked under UAY and 92 research proposals from IITs have been approved. Under this scheme, INR 75 crore have been disbursed for research proposals from IITs under 6 domains.

Smart India Hackathon, under MHRD was conducted on 1 April, 2017. About 7,500 teams from tier 2-3 cities including 40,000+ students, 29 Government Departments participated in the 36-hour non-stop digital programming event.

NIDHI (NATIONAL INITIATIVE FOR DEVELOPMENT AND HARNESSING INNOVATIONS): The 8 components under NIDHI would provide a range of funding support to Startups from idea to market. Ignition grant/award of INR 10 lakhs to be given. Guidelines and proforma for submission of proposals have been published on the website. 19 new TBIs have been established and 9 TBIs supported for Seed Support System (SSS). 10 NIDHI-PRAYAS and 10 NIDHI-EIR have been sanctioned. Also, Grand challenge was conducted to promote entrepreneurship amongst student community. 224 applications were received and out of 30 finalists selected, 12 student-run teams were awarded INR 10 lakhs each.

STATES WITH STARTUP POLICIES: 18 States, viz., Gujarat, Madhya Pradesh, Karnataka, Telangana, Jharkhand, Uttar Pradesh, Odisha, Chhattisgarh, Bihar, West Bengal, Uttarakhand, Andhra Pradesh, Rajasthan, Kerala, Goa, Haryana, Assam and Punjab have formulated Startup Policies since October 2014.

As on 1 December, 2017, a total of 5,350 Startups have been recognised by Department of Industrial Policy and Promotion (DIPP) for availing benefits under Startup India initiative.

The status of the financial assistance provided through Fund of Funds for Startups (FFS) under the Startup India initiative is as follows:

- INR 500 crores have been released to SIDBI in Financial Year 2015-16 and INR 100 crores in Financial Year 2016-17.
- Total commitments under FFS by SIDBI are at INR 605.7 crores to 17 Alternative Investment Funds (AIFs).
- AIFs have drawn INR 90.62 crores from the FFS and have invested a total of INR 337.02 crores in 75 Startups.

Out of the applications received, 6,096 have been recognised as Startups by DIPP. 74 Startups have been approved for availing tax benefits by IMB, as of 1st week of January2018.

Number Of Beneficiaries

- 1,835 applications have been received for recognition, out of which 713 had the required documents and have been recognised as Startups by DIPP
- 146 applications could be considered for tax benefits, out of which 10 Startups have been approved by IMB for availing tax benefit
- 270+ Startups have been mentored for incubation

and funding support by Startup India Hub

- 104 applications have received a rebate of up to 80% on patent fees and have also received legal assistance free of cost
- 25 Startups have made a request for expedited examination [Form 18(A)], whereas trademark facilitation has been extended to 47 Startups
- 290 Startups have received benefits from 20 bio-incubators supported by DBT (Department of Bio-Technology)
- 92 proposals from IITs have been recommended for approval for funding support by MHRD, DST and Industry under Uchchatar Avishkar Yojana (UAY)

Startup Policy and Implementation

Government of Andhra Pradesh has developed a Startup policy which is based on 5 pillars; 1. Create world-class shared infrastructure; 2. Support to incubators and accelerators in tier-2 and 3 cities; 3. Develop Human Capital and utilise immense talent pool; 4. Provide funding support of ₹ 100 crores to Startups; and 5. Ensure good governance at the State level.

Government of Uttar Pradesh through its Startup Policy gives thrust on "START IN UP" to nurture startup culture using INFUSE model (Incubators – Fund of Funds – Startup Entrepreneurs).

Various incentives given under the policy are:

- Capital Grant to incubators for up to ₹ 25 lakhs
- ₹ 2 lakhs to mentors associated with incubators
- Monthly Sustenance Allowance of ₹ 15,000 for a period of 1 year

- ₹ 100 crores Fund of Funds for Startups based in Uttar Pradesh

Government of Karnataka has launched a ₹ 10-crore fund for women entrepreneurs, through which the Department of Information Technology, Biotechnology and Science & Technology can sanction up to ₹ 50 lakhs for any woman innovator looking for funds for proof of concept validation, certification, and for other purposes such as to cover costs in manufacturing pilot devices.

Government of Telangana (GoT) on the occasion of Global Entrepreneurship Summit (GES), 2017 has announced the launch of a Venture Capital (VC) fund with a corpus of ₹ 15 crores to fund women entrepreneurs. The fund will invest anywhere between ₹ 25 lakhs to ₹ 1 crore in Startups run by women entrepreneurs supported by I&C Department of GoT.

Government of Haryana in its Startup policy has declared to set up a United Nations Technology & Innovation Lab (UNTIL) in collaboration with United Nations to promote women entrepreneurship and digital literacy in the State. The objective is to build a strong ecosystem of 50 women-led Startups by 2019 and target USD 5 million in fund-raising for women technology Startups in 5 years.

Government of Andhra Pradesh (AP) has established AP Innovation Society to create a world-class innovation ecosystem, promote Startups in the State and inculcate Innovation among people. It drives innovation through a four-tier model, viz., Government Tier, University Tier, Industrial Tier and Rural or Urban Tier.

Government of Rajasthan has launched an online platform 'iStart' to build an environment to have an easy access to knowledge exchange and funding. The Startups can register to apply for several programmes, incentives under the Rajasthan's Startup initiative. The registered Startups are provided with a scorecard based on the pitching deck submitted by the applicant. Further, customised offerings include 1 month boot camp, mentor and investor connect.

Government of Chhattisgarh under its Startup initiative has forged partnerships with Wadhwani Foundation's National Entrepreneurship Network (NEN) for conducting workshops, mentoring sessions and college outreach. Other partners include Intel, Kauffman's foundation and Peacetech Labs, US.

Government of Gujarat has created 'Gujarat Venture Fund Limited (GVFL) Startup Fund' of ₹ 250 crores towards promoting Startup ecosystem.

Government of Gujarat organised Vibrant Gujarat Startup Summit, 2016. It was a two-day event of experiential networking and learning for Startups. The event included workshops and speaker sessions on topics critical to innovation, targeted specifically at the interests, challenges and opportunities of entrepreneurs.

Bihar Startup Yatra is a State-wide effort to foster entrepreneurship and help Startups (organised by Bihar Entrepreneurs' Association in association with Department of Industries, Government of Bihar). 13 such Yatras have been successfully conducted at various institutes in Bihar, such as SJS College, Arwal; Patna Science College; RBS College, Samastipur; and Nalanda University among others.

Thus, the StatUp India initiative has built a strong eco-system for nurturing innovation and entrepreneurship. This measure of the Government is helping to create large-scale job opportunities across the sectors and accelerate the economic growth of the country.

❒

13
Standup India

Standup India was launched by Prime Minister Narendra Modi on 5 April 2016 to support entrepreneurship among women and SC & ST communities.

The Standup India scheme aims at promoting entrepreneurship among women and scheduled castes and tribes. The scheme is anchored by Department of Financial Services (DFS), Ministry of Finance, Government of India.

Source: *https://www.standupmitra.in*

Standup India Scheme facilitates bank loans between ₹ 10 lakhs and ₹ 1 crore to at least one Scheduled Caste (SC) or Scheduled Tribe (ST) borrower and at least one woman borrower per bank branch for setting up a greenfield enterprise. This enterprise may be in manufacturing, services or the trading sector. In case of non-individual enterprises, at least 51% of the shareholding and controlling stake should be held by either an SC/ST or woman entrepreneur.

Eligibility:

- SC/ST and/or woman entrepreneurs, above 18 years of age.
- Loan under the scheme is available for only greenfield project. Greenfield signifies, in this context, the first-time venture of the beneficiary in the manufacturing or services or trading sector.
- In case of non-individual enterprises, 51% of the shareholding and controlling stake should be held by either SC/ST and/or Women Entrepreneur.
- Borrower should not be in default to any bank/ financial institution.

The broad features of the scheme are as under:

- Composite loan between ₹ 10 lakhs and up to ₹ 100 lakhs, inclusive of working capital component for setting up any new enterprise.
- Debit Card (RuPay) for withdrawal of working capital.
- Credit history of the borrower to be developed.
- Refinance window through Small Industries Development Bank of India (SIDBI) with an initial amount of ₹ 10,000 crores.

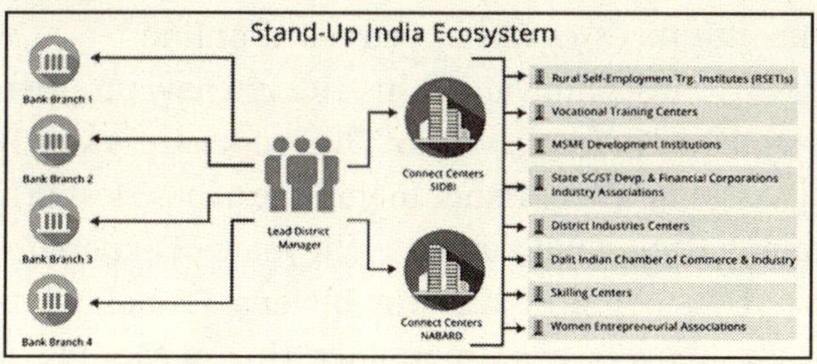

Source: *https://www.startupindia.gov.in*

- Creation of a corpus of ₹ 5,000 crores for credit guarantee through NCGTC.

- Handholding support for borrowers with comprehensive support for pre-loan training needs, facilitating loan, factoring, marketing, etc.
- Web Portal for online registration and support services.

The total number of entrepreneurs who have been extended loan facility under the Standup India Scheme in 2016 was 21,735 and the total amount sanctioned was ₹ 4,747.95 crores. The percentage-wise break-up was Scheduled Caste (SC) – 15.05%, Scheduled Tribe (ST) – 4.28% and Women – 80.67%.

The number of loans given by Public Sector, Private and Regional Banks under the Standup India Scheme is 51,888, 2,445, and 1,009, respectively up to 07.03.2018 since the inception of the scheme.

Regional Rural Banks have sanctioned 180 loans to borrowers of Scheduled Castes (SC) category as on 07.03.2018 since the inception of the scheme.

Startup India programme is a comprehensive action plan to foster entrepreneurship and promote innovation. It aims to minimise the regulatory burden and provide support to start-ups. Over 1,200 redundant laws have been scrapped, 87 rules for FDI have been eased in 21 sectors, and several government processes have been taken online.

M/s Sri Durga Bhavani Industries is a new proprietorship firm established in August 2016. The Proprietress Mrs. Boyena Sridevi has gained experience in this line of business in finance and administration with about eight years of experience. She is assisted by her husband Mr. Boyena Ramakrishna Rao. He has got knowledge in manufacturing of Moulds, Rubber and Plastic, Jigs and Fixtures and Precision components of Automobile sector. Considering the growth prospects, the promoters have planned to establish a unit for manufacture of Rubber and Plastic Moulds, Jigs and Fixtures, all types of Precision components and Automobile components.

A term loan of ₹ 90.00 lakhs and a cash credit limit of ₹ 10 lakhs was sanctioned on 28.09.2016 under Standup India Scheme. The firm is expected to record a turnover of ₹ 20 lakhs till March 2017 and in FY 2017-18, it is expecting a turnover of ₹ 120 lakhs. The women entrepreneurs not only added to the growth of MSME sector but also provided employment to many people, thus adding to the GDP growth of the country in many ways.They have therefore, justified the name given "Standup India" to the scheme.

Smt. Prabha Nautiyal was a homemaker and it was her dream to contribute to the society by proving cost-effective and environment-friendly illumination to households. She formed a limited liability partnership firm on 5 September 2016 along with 2 other partners, viz., Gurdeep Singh and Mamta Taparia. Gurdeep Singh is having more than 20 years of experience in electronic & electrical systems and DG sets while Mamta Taparia is in the business of designing & trading of diamond jewellery and trading of LED lights. With some initial contribution, they intended to set up a factory for the manufacturing of LED bulbs, lights, mobile chargers, etc. The bank sanctioned a credit facility of ₹ 1 crore (term loan of ₹ 75 lakhs and WC of ₹ 25 lakhs) in favour of the company under Stand-up India scheme on 27.10.2016. The borrower has started production in her factory and is running the same efficiently since January 2017.

Thus, the scheme not only provided the shape to the thoughts of a homemakerand turned her to an entrepreneur, but has also contributed towards environmental concern along with providing livelihood to the number of people earning bread from the enterprise. This is a success story of a housewife turning into an entrepreneur. ❒

14
Swachh Bharat

स्वच्छ भारत

एक कदम स्वच्छता की ओर

"Sanitation is more important than independence."

– M.K. Gandhi

Poor sanitation leads to several health-related diseases and untimely deaths. A charity organisation 'WaterAid' had painted a grim situation in one of its reports in 2014. It had then reported that less than a third of India's 1.2 billion people had access to sanitation and more than 1,86,000 children under the age of five used to die every year from diarrheal diseases caused by unsafe water and poor sanitation. It has its economic pitfalls also. It is estimated that the country is losing 6.4% of GDP annually as poor access to sanitation resulting in diseases and deaths.

According to World Health Organization, an average of ₹ 6,500 per person is lost in India due to lack of cleanliness and hygiene.

Swachh Bharat would, therefore, make a significant impact on public health, and in safeguarding income of the poor, ultimately contributing to the national economy.

According to UNICEF, almost half of Indian population

lacks access to a toilet and defecates in the open. The situation is far worse in the rural areas. Even after 70-plus years of independence, 70% of rural population have no access to toilets.

2 October 2014 will go down in the history books as the biggest campaign for "Swachh Bharat" when Prime Minister Modi himself wielded a broom and swept the dirty streets of New Delhi. The people responded to his clarion call to join him in this endeavour to give a fitting tribute to Mahatma Gandhi, who wanted to make sanitation a priority for India more than a century ago.

Launched on 2 October 2014, the Swachh Bharat Mission aims to end the widespread practice of open defecation, build more toilets and improve waste management, among other goals. The Mission aims to achieve a Swachh Bharat by 2019, as a fitting tribute to Mahatma Gandhi on his 150th birth anniversary.

Following are the Objectives:

- Eliminate open defecation.
- Conversion of insanitary toilets to pour-flush toilets.
- Eradication of manual scavenging.
- 100% collection and scientific processing/disposal reuse/recycle of Municipal Solid Waste.
- To bring about a behavioural change in people regarding healthy sanitation practices.
- Generate awareness among the citizens about sanitation and its linkages with public health.
- Strengthening of urban local bodies to design, execute and operate systems.
- To create enabling environment for private sector participation in Capital Expenditure and Operation & Maintenance (O&M) costs.

The Mission has the following components:

- Construction of Household Toilets
- Community and Public Toilets
- Solid Waste Management
- Information, Education & Communication (IEC) and Public Awareness
- Capacity Building and Administrative & Office Expenses (A&OE).

Over 6 crore toilets have been built across rural India under the Mission. Two independent surveys by the Quality Council of India in 2017 and National Sample Survey Organisation in 2016 have pegged the usage of these toilets at 91% and 95%, respectively. As an outcome, over 3 lakh villages and 300 districts have been declared Open Defecation Free (ODF) across ten States and Union Territories, namely Sikkim, Himachal Pradesh, Kerala, Haryana, Uttarakhand, Gujarat, Arunachal Pradesh, Chhattisgarh, Chandigarh and Daman & Diu.

Here are some metrics that indicate the success of Swachh Bharat in rural areas:

- Till date, in rural areas, 696.79 lakh toilets have been built.
- In the last year, i.e., 2017-2018, 297,971,326 toilets have been built.
- There has been a 43.68% increase in households with toilets since 2014.
- 371 districts have been made open defecation-free.
- 1,54,855 Gram Panchayats are now open defecation-free.
- 3,50,342 villages have declared themselves open defecation-free.

In urban areas, Swachh Bharat has focussed on the theme of 3 ₹, i.e., Reduce, Reuse & Recycle. The principle of

3₹ – Reduce, Reuse and Recycle – has been an integral part of Indian culture. Preserving biodiversity, sustainable living and peaceful coexistence with nature hasbeen the guiding philosophy of the Indian way of life and have always been a part of the teachings of ancient scriptures.

Swachh Bharat in urban areas has been equally successful as well. Let's take a look at some of the metrics for urban areas:

- 46,36,158 individual toilets have been constructed.
- 3,06,064 community and public toilets have been built.
- 2,029 cities have been declared open defecation-free.
- 100% door-to-door waste collection in 51,734 wards.
- 88.4 Megawatt of energy is being produced from waste.
- 1,64,891.6 metric tonnes of compost have been produced from waste.

The financial allocations under the Swachh Bharat Mission increased from ₹ 2850 crores in 2014-15 to ₹ 6525 crores in 2015-16, to ₹ 10,500 crores in 2016-17, to ₹ 14,000 crores in 2017-18.

In the last 3 years, under the Swachh Bharat Mission, 48,264,304 toilets were constructed. Open Defecation-Free Villages reached 2,38,966. Individual toilet coverage increased from 42% in 2014 to 64% in 2017.

An innovative monitoring and evaluation system was put in place. The Swachh Sarvekshan was conducted for rural India and revealed that Mandi (Himachal Pradesh) and Sindhudurg (Maharashtra) were the cleanest districts in India. The Swachh Sarvekshan assessed 22 Hill districts and 53 Plain areas. National-level monitors were hired to carry out sample-based checks of sanitation coverage and open defecation-free status across the country.

A massive survey covering 92,000 households in 4,626 villages across the country is being conducted. An additional 200 villages located on the banks of Ganga are being surveyed. An eminent personality like Amitabh Bachchan was nominated as the Brand Ambassador for Swachh Bharat Mission and celebrities like Sachin Tendulkar and Akshay Kumar attended champion collector conclaves for motivational purposes. The Swachh Bharat Mission maintained a significant social media engagement for enhancing awareness levels and a newsletter Swachhta Samachar Patrika was published on a regular basis.

Following is a list of few initiatives led collectively by the government and citizen groups, which have led to large-scale changes and taken India a step towards becoming more 'swachh'.

The women and children of Brahmpura village in Darbhanga, one of the most backward districts of Bihar, no longer step out to defecate in the open. This has been made possible because of the successful and replicable model formulated by Anand Jha and his team that has helped build over 1,500 toilets in seven villages across the district. Anand and his wife, Nivedita, with the help of the then district magistrate, who assured timely reimbursements, decided to start constructing the toilets for the poor with their own money. Within the first month itself, toilets were built for 100 families. The Brahmpura model was adopted by all 550 villages of the Darbhanga district until every village was declared open defecation-free.

Construction of Public Toilets: The Directorate of Municipal Administration (DMA) of Tamil Nadu has designed the Namma Toilet (Our Toilet) to address the most basic needs of ventilation, natural light, safety and privacy. The Namma toilets are user-friendly, durable and vandal-resistant.

The design of such toilets has taken into consideration the feedback received from households and experts through discussions. Based on this, standardised terms and conditions of the tender were prepared and sent to all ULBs in the state. Since the DMA did not receive a response from the sufficient number of bidders, ULBs were advised to move ahead with the conventional method of construction through Engineering Procurement Contract (EPC).

The estimated cost of the toilet is ₹ 15 lakhs per unit with 8 seats. Presented below is the progress:

- Total number of sanctioned Namma Toilets till date: 531
- Completed toilets and put into use till date: 98
- Toilets in progress: 122
- Number of tenders cancelled and new tender called under conventional method: 330
- The Namma toilets are being constructed through EPC. About 50% of the toilets are operated and maintained by the contractors and the remaining 50% are being operated and maintained by the ULBs. The O&M costs of the toilets are borne by the respective ULBs. There is no user fee.

In East Khasi Hills District, under Pynursla C&RD Block, Thiebskai is a village under the Raid Rangnath of Hima Khyrim, a small, captivating, solitary village with 21 households and an SSA (Sarva Shiksha Abhiyan) School. The people of this village practice broom grass cultivation as the main source of their livelihood besides bay leaf and black pepper. On 30 July 2015, Thiebskai embraced a journey of transformation. It is on this day that the village envisaged a new picture for their future. It is a brave, well-thought decision that the village took to set on this journey to transform their village into a

Clean & Healthy Sanitary one. It can be proudly said that the village did not venture this mission alone, but with the proper assistance & guidance of the Block coordinator and field-workers of Swatch Bharat Mission.

The Coordinator along with the field-workers visited the village and facilitated a brief discussion (pre-triggering phase) leading to the consciousness of the public about the benefit of healthy sanitation and community hygiene in general. The people of Thiebskai decided to make a change and strive for a goal to stop Open Defecation and secure a clean environment. Subsequently, the village formed Village Water & Sanitation Committee (VWSC) of Theibskai for the purpose. Decency, safety and aesthetics were established with the construction of toilets for children and adults in Thiebskei Village. In a period of 7 months, the people achieved the status of ODF and hoisted the Flag of an Open Defecation-Free (ODF) village.

Many of these stories involve women warriors who have come forward to do their bit towards building a Swachh India. From a 12-year-old to a 106-year-old, women from across India are leading the swachhta fight in their own unique ways.

Kunwar Bai, a 106-year-old woman from Chhattisgarh, became the face of open defecation movement in the state after she sold off her goats, the only source of earning money to build two toilets at home. Later, she started counselling people of her village in Kotabharri on the importance of having a toilet at home. For her Swachh efforts, she was even felicitated by Prime Minister Narendra Modi. Today, both her village and district Dhamtari boast of 100% sanitation.

Kunwar Bai's daughter Sushila Yadav adds, "Because my mother was old, every night, everyday, whenever she used to go out in the open to defecate, she used to fall down. Then, one day under the Swachh Bharat Abhiyan, we were given 15 days' timeline to construct a toilet at home. Rather than taking this as a shock because of the strict timeline, it became an inspiration for my mother. She was fascinated with the concept of having a toilet at home. And that was the beginning of this sanitation revolution. First she decided to sell our goats and get a toilet, and then she started calling other villagers to come by and see that toilet. She would also demonstrate the benefits of having a toilet at home and motivate them to build one."

12-year-old Monidrita Chatterjee has sparked a mini toilet revolution in Jharkhand. Hailing from Jamshedpur, Monidrita from childhood had two dreams – one, to fight open defecation in the country and give other girls the most basic right – a toilet and second, plastic waste management. She saved every penny she could, including the money that she could have splurged during festivals, just to build toilets for girls. In 2016, this little swachh warrior saved ₹ 24,000 and built two toilets for the children of Kendradhi village. Then, she built two toilets in Haldubani village but with a twist – she constructed these toilets with waste products like plastic bottles and fly ash in order to motivate people about recycling plastic.

In Karnataka's Danapur village, there is a Swachh Bharat Fan 'No. 1' – Sharanamma Bakar. She is a vegetable vendor who gives 1 kg tomatoes free to every family that has built a toilet. This is her way to motivate people to construct a toilet at home. This unique idea came to zher when she learnt that around 1,300 families in her village have no access to toilets. Not just this, taking a step forward, Sharanamma also visited households that have toilets just to check whether they are using it or not. Her district Koppal has a little over 50% toilet coverage and is hoping to become Open Defecation-Free soon.

From the woman in Kanpur who sold her 'mangalsutra' to build a toilet to the teenagers in Bihar's Buxar district who gave up wearing gold jewellery until their parents acquiesced and constructed toilets, the movement for a cleaner and safer India is spreading like wildfire.

Women from Brahmpura village in Darbhanga, one of the most backward districts of Bihar, no longer step out to defecate in the open.

In Harayana, Government's 'No Toilet, No Bride' initiative has been so successful that it is common to find the message "I won't allow my daughter to marry into a home without toilets" painted on the walls of the houses.

In Barpeta, Assam, a group of women came together to build toilets. The women skilled themselves to build toilets and to convince 300+ households to build toilets without using Government funds. They ended up saving ₹ 40 lakhs of Government funds.

A host of special initiatives and projects have come out in quick time. The Inter-Ministerial Projects included Swachhta Pakhwadas, Namami Gange, Swachhta Action Plan, Swachh Swasth Sarvatra campaign, School Sanitation drives, Anganwadi Sanitation drives, Railway Sanitation, etc.

The inter-sectoral collaborations included Swachh Iconic Places, Corporate Partnership, Inter-Faith Cooperation, Media engagement and Parliament engagement.

Swachhta Action Plans were developed by 76 union ministries and departments and a web-based portal was developed to monitor progress and highlight implementation status.

Women Swachhagrahis were appointed and Swachh Shakti Awards were instituted to further enhance the participation of women.

The Swachh Bharat success stories said that accessible and secure toilets had made a big difference to the lives of village communities, as they did not have to travel distances in the dark to relieve themselves. Further, the health risks of open defecation were greatly reduced by having a toilet in the house.

Swachh Bharat Abhiyan has become a 'Jan Andolan' receiving tremendous support from the people. Citizens too have turned out in large numbers and pledged for a neat and cleaner India. Taking the broom to sweep the streets, cleaning up the garbage, focusing on sanitation and maintaining a hygienic environment have become a practice after the launch of the Swachh Bharat Abhiyan. People have started to take part and are helping spread the message of 'Cleanliness is next to Godliness'.

By inviting people to participate in the drive, the Swachhta Abhiyan has turned into a National Movement. A sense of responsibility has been evoked among the people through the Clean India Movement. With citizens now becoming active participants in cleanliness activities across the nation, the dream of a 'Clean India' once seen by Mahatma Gandhi has begun to get a shape.

People from different sections of the society have come forward and joined this mass movement of cleanliness. From government officials to jawans, Bollywood actors to the sportspersons, industrialists to spiritual leaders, all have lined up for the noble work. Millions of people across the country have been day after day joining the cleanliness initiatives of the government departments, NGOs and local community centers to make India clean. Organising frequent cleanliness campaigns for spreading awareness about hygiene through plays and music is also being widely carried out across the nation. ❐

15
Infrastructure Development – Roadways & Waterways

Good-quality infrastructure is critical to sustainable growth, especially for rural areas. As over 60% of the population lives in rural areas, with low levels of per capita income, there is need to impart greater attention in improving rural infrastructure. Currently, the rural infrastructure is inadequate to support over 6,00,000 villages. Investment in rural transport infrastructure stimulates the rural economy and, hence, acts as a tool for poverty reduction. The services in the rural sector, like market access, education, health and communication depend on the availability of infrastructure. A common observation has been that the rural areas with better connectivity also lead on the development scale. Inadequate transport infrastructure in rural areas causes lack of mobility and constraint to rural development.

Poor infrastructure has been a major issue for private investment as well as foreign investment in India. To address these infrastructure bottlenecks, the budget has given adequate focus on roads, electricity and digital infrastructure.

This chapter will majorly focus on the development of roadways.

Under the Pradhan Mantri Gram Sadak Yojana (PMGSY),

construction of roads reached 133 km of roads per day in 2016-17, as against an average of 73 km during the period 2011-2014. The allocation under the scheme has been increased to ₹ 19,000 crores in this budget.

The Budget 2017-18 is heavily focused on the infrastructure sector with the aim of "efficiency, productivity and quality of life". To achieve these goals, a total allocation of ₹ 3,96,135 crores has been made, which is 18.45% of the total budgetary allocation and 14% higher than the previous year's budget.

For the road sector, the Budget allocation has increased to ₹ 64,900 crores in 2017-18 from ₹ 57,976 crores in BE 2016-17 (Table 2), which is 27% of the total allocation of the transport sector. It has been proposed that this amount will be spent on various important ongoing projects and programmes and with the new target of a total of 2,000 km of coastal connectivity roads which have been identified for construction and development. This will facilitate better connectivity with ports and remote villages.

Also, the total length of roads, including those under PMGSY, built from 2014-15 till the current year is about 1,40,000 km, which is significantly higher than the previous three years.

The Pradhan Mantri Gram Sadak Yojana (PMGSY) is being implemented as never before and is accelerating an excellent momentum. The pace of construction of PMGSY roads has accelerated to almost double and reach 133 km of roads per day in 2016-17, which is commendable, as against an average of 73 km during the period 2011-2014. The government has also taken up the task of connecting habitations with more than 100 persons in left-wing extremism-affected blocks. The current target under PMGSY is committed to complete by

2019 and to complete this ambitious and important task, a sum of ₹ 19,000 crores in 2017-18 has been allocated for this scheme. The scheme together with the contribution of States, an amount of ₹ 27,000 crores will be spent on PMGSY in 2017-18.

Cabinet has approved a special project for Road Connectivity Project for Left Wing Extremist Areas (RCPLWE) in December 2016. Out of 340 roads of 5,411.81 km and 126 bridges approved by the Cabinet, 268 roads of 4,134.69 km and 181 bridges were also sanctioned in 2017-18.

Works in these areas are likely to be completed by 2020. This is over and above the special provision for 100-249 population villages in 267 LWE Blocks, where work is likely to be completed by 2020.

PMGSY not only strives to build roads but good-quality roads. The inbuilt framework of Quality Management mechanism in PMGSY is a combination of in-house quality control measures and independent verification at state and national levels. 39,811 inspections by State Quality Monitors (SQMs) and 9,204 inspections by National Quality Monitors (NQMs) at the National level were done in 2017-18. This intensified monitoring has impacted quality grading positively; 13.98% completed roads were graded as unsatisfactory in 2013-14, the quality of roads has improved substantially in 2017-18 with 7.46% completed roads graded as unsatisfactory.

As a measure of transparency and accountability, the scheme has put in place a Citizen Feedback system through the MeriSadak App. Out of 25,414 complaints/feedback related to PMGSY, final replies have been sent in 24,791 (97%) cases.

"Green Technologies" have been encouraged for climate-resilient roads in PMGSY. There has been wide acceptability of these technologies. In the last few years, 33,888 km of road length has been sanctioned and 17,785 km of road length has been constructed. During the financial year 2017-18, a record length of 6,313 km has been constructed using green technologies. Rajasthan, Odisha, Madhya Pradesh, Tamil Nadu, Uttar Pradesh, West Bengal and Jharkhand are using this in building green PMGSY roads.

Maintenance of roads, assets created under PMGSY is a big focus for the Ministry and through various advocacy workshops, etc. Rural Road Maintenance policies have been framed for 23 States. Maintenance software eMarg used in Madhya Pradesh will be replicated in all states to streamline maintenance systems of rural roads. A pilot project was initiated by the Ministry to involve SHGs in road maintenance. Uttarakhand Rural Roads Development Agency (URRDA), under the guidance of National Rural Roads Development Agency (NRRDA), initiated Community Contracting for "Off-Carriageway Maintenance" in rural roads through the registered all-Women Mahila Mangal Dal (MMD). Community contracting for road maintenance is not only used as a tool for empowerment of women, it also empowers the community to maintain roads especially in hilly terrains. This model has been successfully tried in Badwani District of Madhya Pradesh as well.

The Special Accelerated Road Development Programme for the North-Eastern Region (SARDP-NE) is aimed at developing road connectivity between remote areas in the North-Eastern region with state capitals and district headquarters – a three-phase project facilitating connectivity of 88 district headquarters in the North-Eastern states to the nearest national highways. This is by far the most ambitious road development programme for the NER. NHAI, state PWDs and the Border Roads Organisation (BRO) are the implementing agencies.

The objectives are as follows:

- Upgrade National Highways connecting state capitals to two/four-lane.
- To provide connectivity of all 88 district headquarter towns of the NER by at least two-lane road.
- Provide road connectivity to backward and remote areas of the NER.
- Improve roads of strategic importance in the border area.

This programme has been envisaged to be taken up under three parts as under:

1. Phase 'A' of SARDP-NE approved by the Government envisages improvement of about 4,099-km length of roads (2,041 km of NH and 2,058 km of State roads). Till August 2015, 2,989 km of length has been sanctioned and 1,565 km of road has been completed. The SARDP-NE Phase 'A' is expected to be completed by March 2017.

2. Phase 'B' of SARDP-NE covers 3,723 km (1,285 km NHs and 2,438 km of State roads) of road. Phase 'B' SARDP-NE shall be taken up after completion of Phase 'A', which is targeted for completion by March 2017.

3. The Arunachal Pradesh Package for Road & Highways involving development of about 2,319 km length of road (1,472 km of NHs & 847 km of State/General Staff/Strategic Roads) has also been approved by the Government. Projects on 776 km are to be taken up on BOT (Annuity) mode and the remaining are to be developed on an item rate contract basis. Till August 2015, 1,552 km of length had been sanctioned and 230 km of the road has been completed. The entire Arunachal Pradesh Package is targeted for completion by March 2018.

Development of Waterways:

A sound and efficient transport infrastructure is the key to boosting economic growth and, in turn, to alleviating poverty and promoting sustainable development. Inland water transport system ensures both, by way of providing access, mobility and connectivity and generating employment at the grassroots with lesser environmental footprint and cost.

India is a land of rivers. It has 7500-km long coastline with approximately 14,500 km of navigable waterways. This offers a huge potential for developing a cheaper and greener mode of transport. But only a very small percentage of trade is currently being carried out through these waterways and coastlines. Coastal shipping accounts for only 6% and inland water transport for about 0.4% of trade.

Nearly 60% of goods today are transported l by congested roads and 25% by rail networks. This slows down the movement of cargo, adds to uncertainties, increases the costs of trade, and leaves deep environmental footprints. It has been found that logistics costs in India account for about 18% of the country's GDP, which is much higher than China, USA, UK and many other countries. This makes Indian goods costlier and, hence, less competitive. As per World Bank analysis, the cost of transport of one tonne of freight over a km by road is ₹ 2.28, by rail ₹ 1.41 and ₹ 1.19 for waterways. So, logistics costs in the country can be brought down considerably by transporting more and more goods by waterways.

In this era of the energy crisis, waterways have been found to be a fuel-efficient, environment-friendly and cost-effective mode of transport, besides having the capacity to ease pressure on rail and road sectors. Inland Waterways Authority of India (IWAI), which came up in October 1986, acts as the nodal agency for optimum utilisation of the vast untapped potential of our inland waterways.

Under the National Waterways Act, 2016, 111 inland waterways have been declared as National Waterways (NWs) in addition to the five existing NWs, across 24 States for utilising them as an environment-friendly and sustainable mode of transport.

Out of these 111 NWs, the following waterways are operational:

(i) NW-1: Ganga-Bhagirathi-Hooghly river system (Allahabad-Haldia).
(ii) NW-2: River Brahmaputra.
(iii) NW-3: West Coast Canal (Kottapuram-Kollam) along with Udyogmandal and Champakara Canals.
(iv) NW-68: Mandovi.
(v) NW-97: Sundarbans waterways.
(vi) NW-111: Zuari

The Jal Marg Vikas Project has been commissioned for capacity augmentation of NW-1 (River Ganga) from Haldia to Varanasi with an objective to facilitate movement of 1,500-2,000 tonne vessels. The project has been undertaken with the technical and financial support of the World Bank at an estimated cost of ₹ 4,200 crores. The project is scheduled to be completed in six years. Under this project, various sub-projects include fairway development and construction of multimodal terminals at Varanasi, Sahibganj and Haldia and a new navigation lock at Farakka. On NW-2 (River Brahmaputra), a Ro-Ro service has started and a ship repair facility is being constructed at Pandu (Guwahati).

Commencement of development of six more waterways is planned in this financial year. These waterways are NW-4 (Kakinada-Puducherry Canal alongwith Krishna & Godavari Rivers), NW-5 (East Coast Canal with Brahmani & Mahanadi

Delta), NW-16 (Barak), NW-37 (Gandak), NW-40 (Ghagra River) and NW-58 (Kosi). The development of NW-4 & 5 has already been initiated and status is as below:

National Waterway-4

A Memorandum of Understanding (MoU) has been entered into between Inland Waterways Authority of India (IWAI) and Government of Andhra Pradesh to develop the Kakinada- Puducherry canal system along with Krishna and Godavari Rivers in Andhra Pradesh through Special Purpose Vehicle (SPV) to be formed by the Government of Andhra Pradesh and IWAI. Feasibility studies, including delineation of land, have also been undertaken. The fairway stretch between Vijayawada and Muktiyala (87 km) is being developed through dredging for which tenders have been floated by IWAI. This will help to move the cement required for construction of the new capital of Andhra Pradesh at Amravati.

National Waterway-5

NW-5, with a total length of 588 km, consists of river & canal portion, i.e, East Coast Canal. The development of river stretch of 333 km consisting of Brahmani, Kharsuanand Delta River Systems of Mahanadi & Brahmani has been taken up initially in two phases. The stretch (between Pankopal to Dhamraand Paradip port) of 203 km is being developed under the 1st phase. Fairway development which includes dredging and setting up of terminal facilities at Pankopal, Paradip and Dhamra are under progress.

River Ganga occupies a special place in the social, cultural and environmental milieu of our country. The Inland Waterways Authority of India (IWAI) follows the principles of 'working with nature' to protect the river's diverse fauna and aquatic biodiversity. For this, minimum dredging is being undertaken for the passage of large barges carrying up to 2,000 tonnes of cargo. In places where large shoals and islands exist, temporary structures of natural materials like bamboo are only used to channelise the water. IWAI is also ensuring that water traffic does not impact the two aquatic wildlife sanctuaries that fall along this stretch of the river – the Kashi Turtle Sanctuary at Varanasi and the Vikramshila Dolphin Sanctuary at Bhagalpur.

IWAI is in the process of developing thirty-seven more NWs in the next three years. Ro-Ro transportation has started between Dhubri and Hatsingamari and slipway facilities are being constructed at Pandu on River Brahmaputra, or NW-2. Normal development works are ongoing on NW-3. The development of NW-4 (Kakinada-Puducherry Canal along with Krishna & Godavari Rivers), NW-5 (East Coast Canal with Brahmani & Mahanadi Delta), NW-16 (Barak), NW-37 (Gandak), NW-40 (Ghagra) and NW-58 (Kosi) also are in progress.

While developing the waterways, the legal framework governing inland waterways vessels is also being revamped. A new Bill is on the anvil to amend the century-old Inland Vessels Act, 1917, in keeping with the needs of the modern inland water transport and the required legal framework. The 2017 Bill addresses the existing lacunae regarding the variation of standards of inland vessels across the states. As per the Draft Bill, Central Government would be the nodal authority to stipulate uniformly applicable standards and measures for safe navigation of inland vessels.

Once fully operational, the integrated system of water-road and rail network will herald a new era of inclusive growth and green economy in India.

❒

16
Ayushman Bharat

In India, 47% of rural citizens and 37% of urban ones borrow money or sell assets to pay medical bills. Medical cost is one of the most common reasons for rural bankruptcy. Bankruptcy caused by medical costs is not limited to India. It is reported that in the United States, close to 40%-50% of all bankruptcies are linked to medical costs.

According to a US government report.

"Overall Economy Rapidly rising healthcare spending is considered to lower the rate of growth in GDP and overall employment, while raising inflation. However, some economists view increases in healthcare spending as a neutral, if not positive, impact on the economy."

A healthy India is a key component for a developed and a financially secure #NewIndia. With this in mind, the Government of India has launched Ayushman Bharat.

Ayushman Bharat is National Health Protection Scheme, which will cover over 10 crore poor and vulnerable families (approximately 50 crore beneficiaries) providing coverage upto 5 lakh rupees per family per year for secondary and tertiary care hospitalisation. Ayushman Bharat – National Health Protection Mission will subsume the ongoing centrally sponsored schemes – Rashtriya Swasthya Bima Yojana (RSBY) and the Senior Citizen Health Insurance Scheme (SCHIS).

Salient Features:

- Ayushman Bharat – National Health Protection Mission will have a defined benefit cover of ₹ 5 lakhs per family per year.
- Benefits of the scheme are portable across the country and a beneficiary covered under the scheme will be allowed to take cashless benefits from any public/private empanelled hospitals across the country.
- This mission will be an entitlementbased scheme with entitlement decided on the basis of deprivation criteria in the SECC database.
- The beneficiaries can avail benefits in both public and empanelled private facilities.
- To control costs, the payments for treatment will be done on package rate (to be defined by the Government in advance) basis.
- One of the core principles of this mission is co-operative federalism and flexibility to states.
- For giving policy directions and fostering coordination between Centre and States, it is proposed to set up Ayushman Bharat – National Health Protection Mission Council (AB-NHPMC) at apex level chaired by Union Health and Family Welfare Minister.
- States would need to have State Health Agency (SHA) to implement the scheme.
- To ensure that the funds reach SHA on time, the transfer of funds from Central Government through Ayushman Bharat – National Health Protection Mission to State Health Agencies may be done through an escrow account directly.
- In partnership with NITI Aayog, a robust, modular, scalable and interoperable IT platform will be made

operational which will entail a paperless, cashless transaction.

Ayushman Bharat – National Health Protection Mission will have major impact on reduction of Out-of-Pocket (OOP) expenditure on ground of:

- Increased benefit cover to nearly 40% of the population, (the poorest & the vulnerable)
- Covering almost all secondary and many tertiary hospitalisations (except a negative list)
- Coverage of ₹ 5 lakhs for each family, (no restriction of family size)

This will lead to increased access to quality health and medication. In addition, the unmet needs of the population which remained hidden due to lack of financial resources will be catered to. This will lead to timely treatments, improvements in health outcomes, patient satisfaction, improvement in productivity and efficiency and job creation, thus leading to improvement in quality of life.

The Government on 1 February, 2018 announced two major initiatives in the health sector, as part of Ayushman Bharat programme that aimed at making path-breaking interventions to address health holistically, in primary, secondary and tertiary care systems, covering both prevention and health promotion.

The initiatives are as follows:

(i) **Health and Wellness Centre:** The National Health Policy, 2017 has envisioned Health and Wellness Centres as the foundation of India's health system. Under this, 1.5 lakh centres will bring healthcare system closer to the homes of people. These centres will provide comprehensive healthcare, including for non-communicable diseases and maternal and child health services. These centres will also provide free essential drugs and diagnostic services. The Budget has allocated ₹ 1200 crores for this flagship programme. The contribution of the private sector through CSR and philanthropic institutions in adopting these centres is also envisaged.

(ii) **National Health Protection Scheme:** The second flagship programme under Ayushman Bharat is National Health Protection Scheme, which will cover over 10 crore poor and vulnerable families (approximately 50 crore beneficiaries) providing coverage up to ₹ 5 lakhs per family per year for secondary and tertiary care hospitalisation. This will be the world's largest government funded healthcare programme. Adequate funds will be provided for smooth implementation of this programme.

These two health sector initiatives under Ayushman Bharat Programme will build a New India 2022 and ensure enhanced productivity, well being and avert wage loss and impoverishment. These schemes will also generate lakhs of jobs, particularly for women.

In order to further enhance the accessibility of quality medical education and healthcare, 24 new Government Medical Colleges and Hospitals will be set up, by upgrading the existing district hospitals in the country. This would ensure that there is at least 1 Medical College for every 3 Parliamentary Constituencies and at least 1 Government Medical College in each State of the country.

Pandit Deendayal Upadhyaya's philosophy of Antyodaya advocates that the development should first begin with the most disadvantaged. Ayushman Bharat is another great example of Antyodaya as it was launched in Bijapur, Chattisgarh – one of the most underdeveloped regions of India.

Starting with Antyodaya, the Central Government now plans to reach Sarvodaya, i.e., wellness for all Indians. Under Ayushman Bharat, the Central Government is setting up 1.5 lakh wellness centres by 2022 that will leverage on comprehensive primary healthcare for preventive, promotive and curative care.

Pradhan Mantri Bharatiya Janaushadhi Pariyojana (PMBJP)

The goal of PMBJP is to provide 'Quality Medicines at Affordable Prices for All'. Prices of many commonly used medicines had become prohibitively expensive due to higher R&D, marketing and distribution costs incurred by pharmaceutical companies.

Talking to reporters in New Delhi, Ananth Kumar, Minister for Chemicals & Fertilisers and Parliamentary Affairs, said that the Government has made health security for all citizens its priority and this aim can only be achieved through the Janaushadhi pariyojana (scheme).

According to a report published in ruralmarketing.in:

Ananth Kumar informed that as on date, 3,000 Pradhan Mantri Bharatiya Janaushadhi Kendra (PMBJK) providing more than 800 medicines are functioning in the country in the 30 States/UTs, covering 426 districts, as compared to only 80 opened between 2008 and 2014. The turnover atthe beginning of the scheme was around ₹ 3 crores, which would increase to around

₹ 60 crores by the end of this year, he informed.

Further, the Minister said that MoUs for opening PMBJKs have been signed by Union Government with 19 State Governments and other organisations/NGOs. A total of 32,225 applications have been received out of which in-principle approval has been given to 30,300 applications.

Talking about the actual reduction in medicine prices, Kumar said that in these PMBJKs, the Government-procured generic medicines are sold, which are 50%-90% less as compared to the branded medicines in open market, for example, the price of Amlodipine 5 mg 10 tablets is ₹ 3.25 as compared to market average price of ₹ 20.00 for branded version.

The Government is making efforts towards future expansion of PMBJKs in the country. The Ministry of Railways has come on board to open Janaushadhi kendras in over 1,000 railway stations across the country in collaboration with Ministry of Chemicals & Fertilisers. Further, the Ministry of Chemicals & Fertilisers has also written to all State Governments to open PMBJKs in District headquarters, Tehsil/Block level, bus stands, etc. to increase the reach of affordable medicines to the poor and underprivileged citizens of the country.

Pradhan Mantri National Dialysis Programme

Every year about 2.2 lakh new patients of End-Stage Renal Disease (ESRD) get added in India, resulting in additional demand for 3.4 crore dialysis every year. With approximately 4,950 dialysis centres, largely in the private sector in India, the demand is less than half met with the existing infrastructure. Since every dialysis has an additional expenditure tag of about ₹ 2000, it results in a monthly expenditure for patients to the tune of ₹ 3-4 lakhs annually.

Besides, most families have to undertake frequent trips, and often over long distances to access dialysis services, incurring heavy travel costs and loss of wages for the patient and family members accompanying the patient. This, therefore, leads to financial catastrophe for practically all families with such patients.

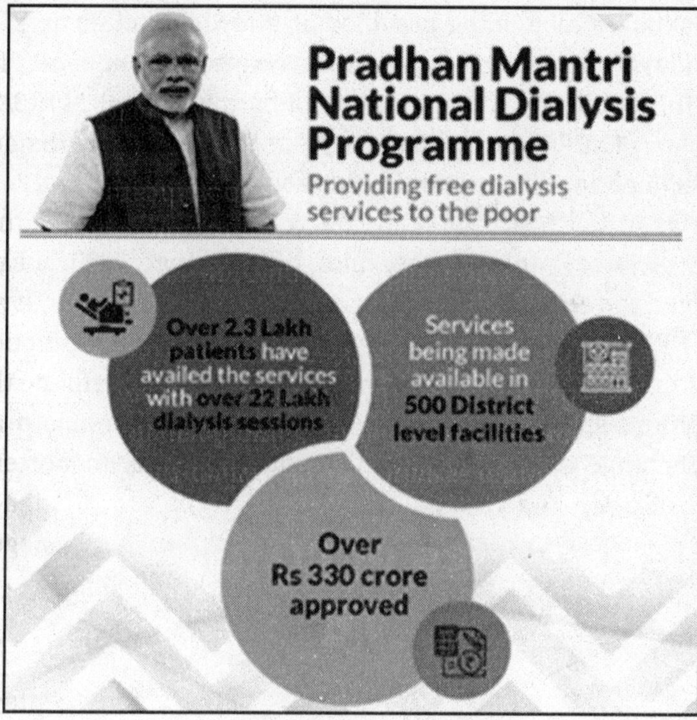

Source: *narendramodi.in*

With the substantial gain in quality of life and extension of progression-free survival for patients, families continue to stretch financially to make large out-of-pocket spends. It has been felt that both in terms of provision of this important life-saving procedure and also for reducing impoverishment on account of out-of-pocket expenditure for patients, a dialysis program is required.

The Central Government has also formulated a National Health Policy to provide quality and affordable healthcare for the poor and middle-class families. Traditional methods such as Yoga and Aryuveda have been integrated as a part of the Central Government's health and wellness programmes.

Over 5,200 life-saving branded medicines and surgical implants are also being provided at affordable rates at 111 Deendayal Amrit Centres across the country.

In addition, the National Pharmaceutical Pricing Authority (NPPA) has capped the price of life-saving coronary stents, a spring-like metal device used to prop open blocked arteries in the heart, at ₹ 30,000, a reduction of 85%. The costs of knee implants have also been capped, which has reduced the cost of a knee replacement surgery by over 70%.

NPPA has capped the prices of 51 essential formulations, including those used for the treatment of cancer, pain, heart conditions and skin problems. The prices have been slashed in the range of 6% to 53%. This move is likely to benefit lakhs of patients across the country.

❒

17
Pradhan Mantri Awas Yojana

Pradhan Mantri Awas Yojana (PMAY), with two components Pradhan Mantri Awas Yojana (Urban) (PMAY-U) for the urban poor and Pradhan Mantri Awaas Yojana (Gramin) (PMAY-G and also PMAY-R) for the rural poor, is an initiative by Prime Minister Narendra Modi in which affordable housing will be provided to the urban poor with a target of building 20 million affordable houses by 31 March, 2022.

Women have been given a preference for the Pradhan Mantri Awas Yojana. The House constructed/acquired should be in the name of the female head of the household or in the joint names of male head of the household and his wife.

Let's see examples of few beneficiaries of PMAY:

Indira E. K., a destitute mother residing with her 9-year-old daughter, stated that PMAY(U) Mission was a blessing in her helpless situation. Indira belongs to scheduled caste community and her education level is too low as she could write her name only. Her husband abandoned her. She does not have requisite skills to find a salaried job, which forced her to do household work. Her earnings were not sufficient to build a home. A strong roof and locked doors remained a dream for her until she heard about PMAY(U). The plight of this woman changed with the enrollment in PMAY(U) project of Thrissur Corporation. She owns 2.8 cent land with property rights which was given to her by her father. Indira was approved as a beneficiary in May 2016 and she constructed 47.69 sq. m. house. She has received ₹ 2.70 lakhs subsidy and completed up to roof level concreting. In her words: "PMAY(U) is a grace from God, which wipes the tears of poor people and provides wings to their shelter dreams."

Jayaben Chavda from Ahmedabad works as a sweeper in the first half of the day and later works as a packer in a jeans-manufacturing company. Together, she earns around ₹ 19,000. Her husband works as a driver and earns ₹ 7000 a month. They have been staying either with relatives or on rent. However, over the years, they have managed to save for their dream home. From their savings, they managed to make a down payment of almost ₹ 4.00 lakhs towards their new home. After this, they were sanctioned a loan of ₹ 7.00 lakhs under PMAY(U) Mission. They have received a subsidy of ₹ 1.81 lakhs. They are now living in a house of their own.

Alka Devi used to live in a kuchcha house with her family in Jharkhand. She is illiterate and widow. She sells vegetables to nurture her family. In this situation, making a permanent house for her was like a dream. After knowing about the PMAY(U), she applied for availing the benefits of the scheme. After the excavation of the foundation, the amount of the first installment was given by the Hon'ble Minister, Urban Development and Housing Department, amounting to ₹ 45,000. She started the construction work, after getting the first installment. She began to see the dream of her pucca house being fulfilled in reality. She worked with full diligence and along with her savings from the sale of vegetables and with the support amount received from the government, she completed the house. Now Alka Devi owns a house in which she lives happily with her whole family.

In the backdrop of India facing a massive urban housing shortage of 18.78 million units, the government took a major reform initiative – "Housing for all by 2022", focusing on affordable/low-cost housing.

This scheme is converged with other schemes to ensure houses have toilets, Saubhagya Yojana electricity connection, Ujjwala Yojana LPG gas connection, access to drinking water and Jan Dhan banking facilities, etc.

Cumulative total number of funded houses approved thus far is 39,25,240 in urban areas including the subsumed RAY scheme and completion of construction of 5 million rural houses by March 2018 and 10 million rural houses by March 2019.

Mishasrunnisa, 36 is a homemaker and her husband works in an un-organised sector in Kannur, Kerala. They have three daughters. Her family belongs to BPL category and owns 3 cents of land. Earlier, they were living in a rental house at a monthly rent of ₹ 6,000, which was consuming a major part of their income. Constructing own house was an unfulfilled dream for her family. PMAY(U) Mission project came as a boon to her. She got approval under the Beneficiary Led Construction (BLC) component of PMAY(U) Mission. She managed to complete the lintel level of her dream home and received installments from the municipality. In her words: "The new house has brought a sense of security to us. It has increased our recognition in the society as well."

Pappamma, 43 and her husband Gopalakrishnan, 46 were living in Vadakkevila division of Kollam Corporation. They belong to SC category. The Kollam Corporation provided them with a 3 cent land under SC land scheme in the year 2014. Then they made a temporary shelter with tarpaulin and wood and lived there. Pappamma works as a housemaid and Gopalakrishnan works in a security company. In 2016, Pappamma got approval under the BLC component of PMAY(U) Mission. Pappamma's wait was finally ended when she managed to complete her roof construction without any financial assistance from banks or other financial institutions. In her own words: "It is a dream come true for us. We have been living on rent through generations."

Women Construction groups and Hollow Bricks Unit – Kerala: Kudumbashree is the state-level nodal agency for PMAY(U) in Kerala. Under PMAY(U) Mission, they have got nearly 30,000 houses approved in the state till date. They have estimated to get an approval of 80,000 houses in 2017-18. Hence, it can be foreseen that there would be a huge demand for construction labour in the State for the construction of these houses. Government of Kerala has given accreditation for women construction groups to undertake construction activities under Local Self-Government Department.

Majority of the beneficiaries are members of Kudumbashree network. Hence, apart from filling the gap between demand and supply side, this will instill a sense of ownership as well. These affordable housing projects under PMAY(U) Mission would be constructed by the trained women construction groups, thereby empowering the women by providing them with a livelihood. A total of 217 women are trained under HUDCO. 400 women are trained and 59 Micro-Contracting Construction Groups have been constituted under Kudumbashree. Work to the quantum of ₹ 51 lakhs has been awarded to the groups. 87 houses have been completed and constructed by these teams.

In its seven decades of journey since independence, the real estate and housing sector has come a long way from early years of restrictive policies, deficient planning and highly inadequate resources, to reach a progressive, planned, organised and reformative stage, facilitating urban transformation and speedy economic growth.

The present government's vision is to ensure long-term inclusive development through good governance and transformative reforms to boost real estate, housing and infrastructure – the vital sectors that hold key to economic development. It is a far cry from early years after independence (1947-64) when not much attention was paid towards housing/urban infrastructure due to lack of resources and staff capacity to design and deliver. But, it was during this period that the government introduced state housing boards, mandated to construct houses for public and laid the ground for planned cities.

Real estate, housing and infrastructure are at the forefront of Modi government's policy to boost the economy and push up growth.

❐

18
Ease of Living

Transformation of a nation begins when the life of every citizen changes for the better. Sarvodaya via Antyodaya, i.e., the benefit for all, starting with the poorest of the poor has been the mantra of the first 4 years of the Narendra Modi government.

It aims to provide a life of dignity for every citizen – a home to stay, access to good infrastructure, financial security and in moments that matter, affordable healthcare for every member of the family.

Prime Minister Narendra Modi has built a foundation of a #NewIndia – a healthy, secure India ready to lead the world.

As we reviewed the policies and programmes of the Narendra Modi government, one quote by Mahatma Gandhi comes to mind:

"In a gentle way, you can shake the world."

There is no better quote to describe the first 4 years of the Narendra Modi government. India has changed for the good. A #NewIndia is being born.

❑❑❑